Remembering Me

A Journey of Self-Discovery and Universal Truths

Dr. Elisa Peavey

Veronica Lane Books

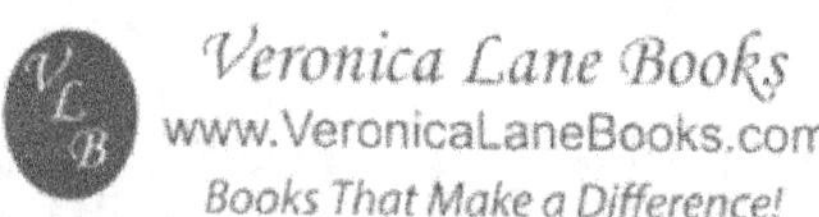

Remembering Me

A Journey of Self-Discovery and Universal Truths

By Dr. Elisa Peavey

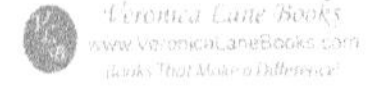

Dedication

Thank you to my mom for always being there, to my dad for showing me dedication and compassion in medicine, to my husband for his undying support, and to my three girls for being my greatest lessons in personal growth. I love you all for eternity.

Introduction

It's been predicted for ages. And talked about it in most religions.

The religion I grew up in called it the Second Coming.

Throughout the centuries, predictions by seers, latter day prophets, and even the Pope himself believe that Jesus of Nazareth will walk among us again in his physical state.

And while I'll tell you he most certainly lived and ascended his lifetime and agree that his consciousness and essence is very much alive today, it is not as many religions would have you believe.

I'll also tell you that much of his teachings, in the modern Bible, were intentionally and contextually changed and mistranslated, as well as the teachings of many others. In 1947 the Dead Sea Scrolls were discovered along with close to 200 copies of books from the Hebrew Bible, representing some of the earliest evidence of biblical text in the world. In contrast to the King James Version, these manuscripts show and confirm different understandings and translations of the same text and script.

Translations which I believe were intentionally changed by an elite few, not wanting us knowing the truth of who and what we truly are. They kept from us the truth of what we're capable of becoming and the truth of the healing potential we all have within.

Much of what is taught in churches and religions around the world contradicts what I've come to know as Universal Law, comprising the ultimate laws that run our Universe. Unfortunately, these contradictions significantly hinder and detour us from our intended spiritual and evolutionary destination.

This knowledge was kept from us to control us financially, morally, and to keep us in fear.

In order to keep us in line.

Throughout the Centuries they've condemned, burned and killed tens if not hundreds upon thousands of witches, wizards, healers, and those talented in apothecary, as being of the devil's work; all in the name of God and Jesus. When in reality those killed were likely gifted intuitives, psychics, shamans, and other healers working closely with God and others in the multidimensional realm.

Unfortunately, religions have used this knowledge to manipulate their constituents.

"If you don't accept Jesus as your Savior, you'll burn in hell forever!"

Pushing the fear deeper and deeper.

I'll explain why most religions have it wrong. About the context and misinformation of religion; that God is out there somewhere, separate from us; judging our sins and punishing us when a mistake is made. I'll also discuss what religions have wrong about Jesus himself.

Who was He truly?

And what were his true teachings and beliefs about God and the Universe?

I know these things better than anyone, and I know them because I am a twin flame to Jesus of Nazareth as He is of me.

Twin flames, meaning fractals from the same OverSoul, the *soul-essence* and inner guidance system we bring with us into each and every lifetime we experience.

I'm also a twin flame to several other famous souls who've lived and died throughout history. Such as Joan of Arc, Elizabeth Taylor, and even Princess Diana, each of us a fractal from the same OverSoul.

And I'm a carrier of the truth of Zero Point Energy, as was Jesus of Nazareth—an energy we all have the ability to tap into and utilize.

I know it sounds crazy, and for a while, I thought maybe I was too.

But this is my story, my truth.

Chapter One

I was born in McCall, Idaho on November 17th, 1978, as the third child and oldest daughter of what would eventually become a family of nine children, six boys and three girls.   As the oldest daughter, by the time I graduated high school, I'd changed more diapers than most and from about seven or eight years old onward, it wasn't uncommon to find me with a younger sibling attached to my hip, my resume for future babysitting gigs.

Like each of us, it was my childhood experiences that shaped and molded the majority of the beliefs, behaviors, and subconscious patterns I've often continued to act out in my life.

The scripts were often helpful in shaping core values, such as the value of hard work, instilled not only by my parents but by a number of adults in my life. Many times, however, the scripts I developed became detrimental to my long-term goals, coming to the forefront and forcing me to deal with them as an adult.

Such as my inherent belief I always have to be in survival mode. Or the belief I developed that earning money and saving it, is impossible.

I've since learned and come to appreciate that between birth to seven years, our mind is like a sponge, spending most of our time in what scientists call the theta state of consciousness. As adults, this is a barely conscious state between sleeping and or after awakening. During these formative years, we're taking in, assessing, and developing belief systems, whether conscious or subconscious, about how the world works, simply by experiencing the environment around us.

Take for example the child who is raised in an environment where the parents have a strict 'children should be seen and not heard' way of child-rearing. The child is taught from a young age that their opinions and voice aren't good enough and they're often taught to suppress and hide their emotions and feelings.

The end result being a child who becomes an adult with difficulties expressing their opinion, thoughts, or emotions for fear of being ridiculed and being told to stop talking. The thyroid gland is emotionally and energetically connected to using one's voice and demonstrating our freedom of choice. When belittled, blocked, or not allowed to speak up and express ourselves, physiologically we shut down and constrict energetic flow to the gland.

This sets into motion a slew of possible issues and health conditions, whether physical, mental, or emotional.

These problems are often due to the dominating influences of the child's environment while in the early developmental stages of their lives.

A child raised in a household where the parents are angry and fight all the time vs a household where they truly communicate their grievances and work to bridge their differences, will raise two entirely different children with two completely different viewpoints and perspectives on life, relationships, love, the value of education, communication, finances, health and more.

For me, the biggest contributors to the deeply held beliefs I had about myself, my abilities, and my dreams came from the experiences I had as a child surrounding our finances, or lack thereof, and the experiences I had growing up in the Latter-day Saints (Mormon) religion, as well as my short-lived basketball career.

Until the age of nine, my childhood consisted of roaming and playing in the forests close to our home, around the creek in the field behind us, finding snakes, frogs, dirt, dinner bells, and above all, everything a child should have when growing up. My dad was a general contractor in McCall, ID during the 80's and until the financial drought of the late 1980s, life was good. Unfortunately, the drought brought little work for my Dad and even less money, forcing my parents to sell the house they'd built for their family and move into our grandfather's rental home.

I distinctly remember my parents' feelings of loss and shame, especially from my Dad. I'm certain had they not suffered such a loss, he most likely wouldn't have changed careers, nor gone back to medical school at the age of 37. Their devastating financial situation was the biggest reason he chose to become a physician, having since helped thousands of patients throughout his career as an OB-GYN.

But the blessing, however, was difficult to see at the time as it was also the start of negative beliefs and thoughts I was developing around money, abundance, and survival. These negative beliefs became a part of my deep psyche, though I had no conscious awareness or knowledge of what was occurring. During my junior high school years, I often had next to nothing in clothes, and at one point I owned only one pair of pants and five t-shirts, which I alternated wearing each day of the week.

The feelings of lack and survival quickly became second nature and soon I was barely aware that my actions, behaviors, thought processes, and patterns were reflecting my subconscious beliefs of lack, shame, and constant survival strategies.

Religion was another major influence in my life, mostly in regard to what a woman's role is (staying home to raise the kids), who carries the priesthood or ability to bless and heal through God, what a proper girl should wear and how she should act, and what happens to us after we die if we are sinners.

Even as a young adult living on my own and into the early years of my marriage, I'd often tell myself, "one day I'll repent from the alcohol I drank, the cigarette I chose to smoke, or the premarital sex I chose to have so I can get into the highest kingdom."

Those deeply ingrained beliefs that my poor choices and sins would dictate my ability to live for eternity with God and my family was keeping me in fear. I was still living in fear.

Raised in a strict Latter-day Saints home, as a teenager I disliked going to church, feeling very much in a box, and hardly resonating with the other kids there. But as a young child, it was a normal and everyday part of my growing up.

The difference between most Latter-day Saints' families and ours was that my mom has always had a close, spiritual connection with God, more so than what's typically accepted or allowed of women in the Latter-day Saints faith. She had full conversations with spirit, sometimes in prayer asking for assistance, and other times in conversation while bartering for an outcome. And from the time I was little, I remember how impressed I always was by her ability to listen inward for answers to her questions. Being a woman of faith, when God spoke, she listened.

I can tell numerous stories she had in close concert with spirit. There was a time that she felt compelled to deliver bread to a random person's house, only to find out later they had nothing to eat.

There was the time, soon after Dad started medical school God told her she was to have another child.

"If I'm meant to have more than one, you'd better send 'em all at once because I can't do this again," she responded.

She said this knowing the most likely outcome.

A week or two later, my Dad was giving her a priesthood blessing when he said, "I command that they…"

He stopped.

"I command that He…"

He stopped.

And through gritted teeth, said, "I command that 'It' be born with a strong mind and strong body."

At the time, my Mom said she clearly knew, there was more than one fetus (verified at her upcoming OB appointment) and she knew they were both boys.

Interestingly, from the earliest time of monitoring and measuring, the twins consistently measured 2 weeks apart in gestational age and of course, they were males, as Mom had prophesized.

Without a doubt, I believe Mom convinced the Universe that twins were the way to go. Her faith, belief, and connection to manifest and direct Spirit was of an incredibly high nature. The Latter-day Saints faith believes only men are allowed to commune and bless others through the power and gift of God. But in truth, it was my Mom who showed, inspired, and taught us that each individual soul has the ability to tap into, connect, speak with, and heal using God's love and healing energy.

While Dad attended medical school, Mom became acquainted with a fellow medical student, skilled in muscle testing and a technique that energetically helped drain "wastes and toxins" from the body. Though we didn't understand what she was doing, or why it seemed to work, whenever someone got sick, my mom would start asking questions. Then she determined what herbs or supplements we needed to take, how much we should take, whether the illness was a virus or other, and if we would benefit from drawing wastes and toxins, sending intentional energy, or both.

My Dad was becoming a doctor, but it was my mom we went to when we were sick. We saved our Dad medical visits for when we needed his skills in suturing, when medications would be beneficial, or when we'd benefit from his medical knowledge and expertise.

The tools Mom developed during this time were a necessary building block on her journey as a healer, and for me to see and witness the benefit of "tapping into" and utilizing the Zero-Point Field, in helping and healing *dis-ease*.

Though, I had *no* idea what we were doing at the time.

As a child, I too had several "psychic and intuitive" moments. At the age of 5, I clearly remember standing in the living room, looking up at my Mom, and saying, "I'm going to be a doctor when I grow up."

"You are?" My Mom replied. "Why is that?"

"Because I'm going to help a lot of people," I said. It felt as simple as that.

When I was 10, I told my Sunday school teacher that she was pregnant and it was a girl, shocking the *bejesus* out of her. But somehow, I just knew.

At the age of 36 my Dad made the choice to go back to school and become a physician. At the time, I was nine years old.

To get the necessary prerequisites, including organic chemistry, we moved from McCall, ID to Boise for a year in 1988 where he also worked for a house-moving and construction company, owned by long-time friends.

In the summer of 1989, with no guarantee of a place to live, my parents moved our family of Mom, Dad, and seven children to Kirksville, MO for Dad to attend KCOM-ATSU, his top choice of medical schools. He could have attended any school he wanted, as he was accepted at every school he applied. Unknowingly, our family would spend the next eight years in what would quickly become our second home and community. When we moved to Kirksville, my parents had seven children and it was during Dad's first year of medical school that Mom became pregnant again, this time with the twins.

Though we wouldn't and couldn't imagine our lives without Daniel and Tyson, their existence added financial strain. My parents came to school with approximately $20,000 in savings, but with the additional medical expenses of their babies' deliveries, the money was gone after a year, and with it the last of their financial reserves.

We were dirt-poor, and though I know my parents did everything possible to save money wherever we could, it was incredibly stressful. Every vacation, from that point on, Dad spent his time doing contractor work, for additional money. When he was a licensed physician, he'd earn the extra money moonlighting, adding to the 80 plus hours he was already working as an OB-GYN resident.

That move was the end of an era, where family vacations became a thing of the past. When once we'd spend a weekend camping, target shooting, or other; any and all time away from school, Dad spent working.

A work pattern and way of life that my Dad would repeat (and one I would eventually adopt) for the next 30-plus years; the mindset and mentality of, "I have to financially take care of my family."

As a child, I understood the necessity, but I also missed having my Dad around—a sentiment I know my brothers and sisters felt as well.

The financial struggle was the worst during my sixth to eighth-grade years. A few times a year, we'd find mysterious boxes of food on our doorsteps, and years later, I learned that our Bishop had called my grandparents, filling them in on our dire situation.

Sports and activities were our escape and in middle school I spent the summers swimming and the winters playing basketball. By high school, I gave up swimming to focus strictly on basketball. I absolutely loved the sport wanting to play in college with a full-ride scholarship.

In the summer of 1995, between my sophomore and junior year in high school, I was playing in a weeklong tournament in southern Missouri. During one of our games, I was running alongside a girl during her fast break. When she jumped for a lay-up, I jumped as well, and I felt the top of my leg turn in one direction, while the bottom leg turned the opposite. When I landed, I knew something wasn't right.

Within 10-15 minutes my knee had swelled to twice the size and I was out from playing for the rest of the week. I returned to Kirksville and saw my orthopedic who after a history, physical exam, and imaging; diagnosed me with an ACL tear. Not wanting to miss playing for a full year, we decided I might do OK with a brace and rehab, as my knee was particularly strong, and even with the physical exam, it didn't act like an ACL tear.

Unfortunately, the injury put me out for two to three months, during which time I gained around 20 lbs. The fault was entirely mine. I've always enjoyed high-quality food, and I was dating a guy whose Mom was an incredible cook. On Sundays, he'd typically join me for dinner at my family's house followed by a visit to his family's house, where there was more food available. And I took advantage!

When the season started in the fall, I resumed my same position as one of the starters. But after a few games and till the end of the season, not only was I not starting, but I was also barely playing a few minutes total if anything at all. I was never sure why this happened, it was very disappointing.

I was beyond devasted. My college basketball dreams felt less and less likely to manifest. Not knowing at that time God knew what was best for me.

In the summer between my junior and senior years, vowing what happened wouldn't happen again, I showed up to every open gym that summer and slowly took off the weight, I'd gained, following my injury.

My senior year started similarly to my junior year; I was one of the starters. But again like the year before, I went from starting to becoming the sixth man, to barely playing at all.

I didn't understand. My parents, and several of my teammates' parents and other adults, would tell me I was the most underestimated player on the team.

Unfortunately, I watched as my dreams of playing in college, scholarship or no, fade away.

It was my first big failure and the first massive hit to my self-confidence, allowing feelings of doubt to slowly creep in.

Unknowingly, I'd spend much of my adult life allowing those low-frequency feelings to overshadow and influence how I felt about myself and my capabilities for achieving success. I didn't realize at the time how many other people allow this to happen in their own lives.

Doing my best to let go of my perceived basketball failures, I began looking toward college without basketball. We lived in the same town as Truman State University, a college collectively known as the "Harvard of the Midwest." Academically, the school was top-notch, in addition, the parties and social events were everything I was looking for and I couldn't wait to move out and become more independent.

Though my parents were averse to me staying in Kirksville, as they'd soon be moving to Oregon, they were supportive of me anyway. As soon as I was able, I found three different jobs to help pay my college tuition, my rent, and my food; working as a lifeguard, waitress, and in a clothing store.

Even with all my financial efforts, money and bills were stressful, and upon graduation from high school, I felt survival mode kick in.

A year later, during the summer of 1998, I realized I wasn't happy in Kirksville, so far from my family.

I'd gained the "freshman 20" and overall missed having the support of my family close by.

In November of 98', while driving home from my waitressing job at the lake, I had an instant thought, a realization, and an *aha* to move closer to my family. It happened that fast and I intuitively knew it was the right choice for me.

One month later, days before Christmas, I drove to Boise, ID in my '94 Ford Tempo, with my brother Ken. And I didn't look back.

One month after that, I started working at DirecTV to save money and get in-state tuition before I started back to school.

Who knew that's where I'd meet my husband?

Chapter Two

If quantum theory were applied to biology on a larger scale, we would be viewed as a complex network of energy fields in some sort of dynamic interplay with our chemical cellular systems. - Lynne McTaggart, *The Field*

In the summer of 2013, after graduating from my medical residency, I took a class called Alchemy. It was a spiritual and self-empowerment class focused on helping us learn the powerful alchemical power we're each afforded in order to transform our own lives, turning everything in it, to gold. Here we faced our demons and dealt with emotional pain or trauma impacting and affecting our daily lives. We underwent multiple spiritual and energetic processes to heal our inner child, learned and grew our energetic gifts, worked together as a community, and underwent processes to heal and cleanse our generational line and DNA.

I was fortunate to take the class with my sister Windy, brother Ryan, two sisters-in-law Krista and Tiffany; and several other people. The timing couldn't have been more perfect as I was ending an important chapter in my life; one as a resident, in training, and making no money. And, I was beginning a new chapter as a family medicine physician-attending in a new job, and with new opportunities. And I dreamed *Big!* I dreamed of owning and creating a massive spiritual and holistic wellness center in the middle of epic nature scape views, equipped for deep healing and spiritual connections. And I figured this class was the perfect start on my journey to acquiring my dreams.

There are three pretty distinct things that stand out about the class itself. I was warned of the potential risk I was to have an issue with alcohol. This was by a 19-year-old beautiful native American boy who was taking the class with his twin sister. We were assigned to practice our intuitive gifts—which we all have in some form—with different people in the class. He went first as the psychic reader. He said, "I see a wine glass and I am feeling the need to warn you to be careful of how much and how often you're drinking. It could become a problem." This, in and of itself, was shocking as I hadn't shared with anyone how often I had been drinking, as of late, and I had begun to question whether I was drinking too much. This is a thought I'm told many alcoholics have throughout their drinking careers.

The second thing I remember being told, in the same psychic read with the same reader, was that I was a bridge between Western medicine and other integrative/alternative therapies for healing and that I would be a part of creating a *New* way of medicine.

Thirdly, I was told by the facilitators, who were all gifted intuits and psychics, that I was a group facilitator, a spiritual leader, a speaker, and a healer.

I had no idea what that meant but I envisioned that maybe I would become someone similar to Deepak Chopra, Wayne Dyer, Louise Hay, or Dr. Christine Northrup. These were my heroes who I had come to know, read, and cling to when times were difficult, or to use as examples for patients, looking for non-traditional therapies to treat their illnesses or conditions. I had no idea how or if this would ever come about, but occasionally over the next several years, I would have snippets of visions of me working alongside some of the great spiritual leaders of our time.

Lastly, what I remember most is what I pictured, in my minds-eye, when asked what I see when picturing my spiritual or higher self. What I saw was a being of pure light, dressed in white with a radiance of bright light bursting from me, intermingled with subtle but distinct hues of purples, blues, and pinks coming from my entire body with hands outstretched, palms facing up with a halo of light surrounding me. I had the immediate feeling and impression that it was Jesus of Nazareth, similar to several of the paintings with him standing, his hands turned out.

At the time, I was immediately confused and responded by saying, "All I see is a big bright light," refusing to describe what I felt I was truly seeing—me as an image of Jesus.

I remember telling myself: I'm all *heart* as he himself was, and that I'm a healer as well. But, during this week I'd also come to the realization that Jesus's incredible healing abilities came from his perfect use and understanding of the Universal Laws. He knew how to tap into Zero Point Energy and thus became the perfect conduit for healing.

The Zero Point Energy Field is so named due to the fluctuations in atomic particles observed when the temperatures are absolute zero, or the lowest energy state, where nothing is supposed to occur.

At this state, Zero Point Energy is available to each of us, in order to tap into it for answers, for *free* energy, and most importantly for healing; physically, emotionally, and spiritually.

Zero Point, in essence, is God. It's the Field, the Matrix, the Container. And though we can't typically see or feel it, the Field is 96% of what's around and within us. The other 4% of the Universe is the matter, or what we can physically see. For definitional purposes, matter is anything solid, from rocks and plants to animals, humans, and the planets and stars in the Universe—all energetically connected, via the Zero Point Field.

If the Field were removed from within us, removed from all matter and the matter was compacted together, it would compact to the size of a little green pea. Exactly as it was moments before the Big Bang, shattering the matter into multiple different directions and transformations.

The Zero Point Field is the ethereal medium interconnecting all matter, created at the time of the Big Bang, at the time that the *One* (God) fractalized Himself into an innumerable number of OverSouls, our higher selves, the *soul-essence* we take with us into every life experience we have. He fractalized himself so that He too could continue to learn and grow.

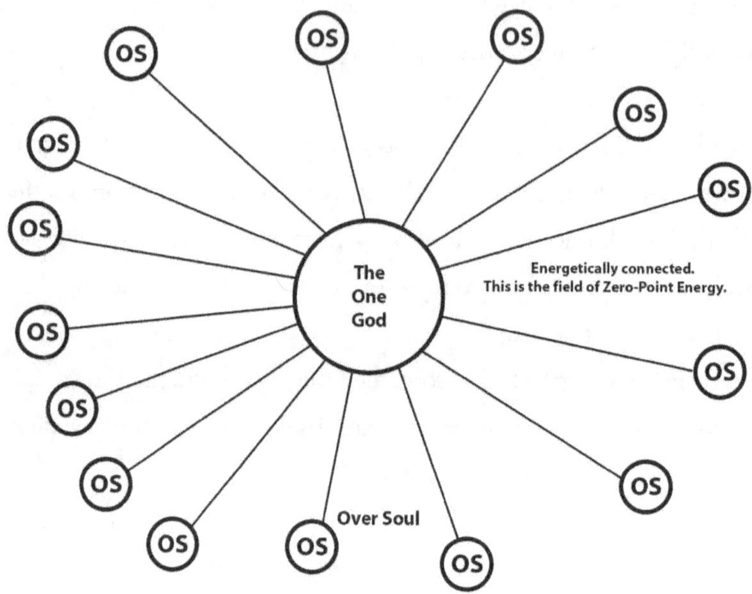

At the time of Big Bang, the "One" divided into billions, if not trillions of fractals called Over-Souls. Each Over-Soul fuses with matter at this time.

Zero Point is also responsible for the stability of all matter. If it didn't exist, all subatomic matter and structures would cease to exist; and all matter would collapse.

This means that we, the stars, our pets, our families, the trees, Mother Nature, the planets—*everything that is will fail to exist.*

At a fundamental, subatomic level, there is no mass, no matter; we're simply a bunch of subatomic particles vibrating...meaning that we're all energy, all electromagnetic charge.

Zero Point is the *field* that is energetically connected to each of us, within us; moving through us and connecting us to everything else. The Field experiences every success and every struggle, every laugh, and every tear. It's in essence a documentation and recording of everything that happens in the Universe...past, present, and future.

The Zero Point Field is also beyond our concepts of time and space.

We can interchange the terms Zero Point and God. All the while God is experiencing through us; Himself continuing to evolve and spiritually grow..Zero

Point is also a state of consciousness; an energy and healing access point that we are all capable of accessing and tapping into.

No subatomic particle (matter) is ever completely at rest as there is always a ground state of energy—the Zero Point Energy Field constantly interacting with it. This interplay on a small scale produces minute amounts of energy. But on a grander universal level, the energy it produces is more than what's found in all the matter of all the multiverses beyond imagination. In one single transaction, the energy produced is half a photon's worth of light but add them up and we have access to a vast, indispensable, and inexhaustible supply of free energy. This energy is equal to or greater than the power of an atomic nucleus, or as physicist Richard Feynman said, "The energy in a single cubic meter of space is enough to boil all the oceans of the world."

In other words, *free*, boundless, non-polluting energy is available to every and anyone who wants to access it. The question is, are we interested in this energy? What are we willing to do to experience it, and how do we start?

Learning to access the Zero Point Field is something I intuitively knew at the time that we were all *capable* of doing. I also knew these were the messages and teachings Jesus of Nazareth wanted everyone to know, and which I believe were intentionally mistranslated in the Kings James version of the Bible.

This idea that we're separate from God, from each other, or the idea that *only* through a belief in Christ or God may one find salvation and redemption I believe is absolutely incorrect. I know the wordS the bible speaks have been changed from their original wording, their meanings changed for the benefit of the 16th-century bible.

An example of this is when the word *kaneh bosem* was changed to the word calamus in 333 AD when the Hebrew Bible was converted into Greek. *Kaneh* in Hebrew means reed, calamus, or cane and *bosum* meaning perfume, scent, or fragrance. Put them together and *kaneh bosem* became *kannabus* in Hebrew, their term for hemp. But instead, the word was changed to *calamus*, a plant called the *Acorus calamus of Linnaeus*, that while it smells wonderful, has far fewer healing and medicinal benefits. Unfortunately, calamus has replaced hemp in several passages throughout the Bible.

Exodus 30:23 is the recipe for the Holy Anointing Oil, including calamus in the recipe. However, doesn't it make more sense for it to be hemp? An herb known about and used for medicinal and spiritual purposes through the centuries versus a plant with less medicinal benefit but a lot of fragrance? My mom makes the Exodus Oil recipe using hemp and its by far one of the best oils for pain, menstrual cramps, scrapes and contusions, joint pain, musculoskeletal inflammation and other injuries.

I remember having one lady use it for menstrual cramps so severe she could hardly sit up straight. She put the oil in her belly button (quick access to the venous and circulatory system) and rubbed it all over her stomach. Within 15 minutes her cramps were completely gone which she claimed had never occurred in such a quick amount of time.

In the 20th Century, it was Rockefeller and others, such as the paper industry, who smeared cannabis into the ground, claiming it a Schedule 1 drug and massively dangerous. One year after it was made illegal, cannabis was listed in the magazine, *Popular Mechanics*, as the new "billion-dollar crop" due to its incredible versatility as a medicine, a textile, and over 1000 other amazing uses.

Unfortunately, over the next 70-plus years the pharmaceutical and medical industries inundated and brainwashed us to believe cannabis was dangerous and addictive. Keeping millions from using it and instead promoting and prescribing more dangerous and exponentially more addictive medications such as opioids and benzodiazepines.

The Bible was mistranslated for control, done to keep the masses of people from having access to and/or knowing the truth and power of what we are, similarly to what occurred with cannabis. They hid the truth of this powerful medicine, as its a competitor in multiple industries and they wanted to control the pharmaceuticals, the paper industry, their pockets, and ultimately us.

In truth, we're each divine beings. Every. Single. One. Of. Us. Of course, we're at different stages of spiritual development and evolution. In addition, we're energetically and divinely connected, to each other, to our animals, to nature, to the stars, and *most* importantly—to God! These connections began at the moment of the Big Bang when God in spirit came together with form and became an innumerable number of fractals of Himself.

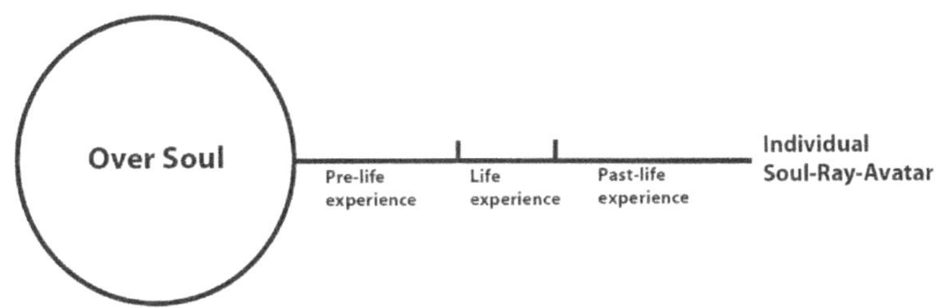

Meaning we're all Gods. Each divine beings, at different levels of experience and spiritual advancement. At the time of the Big Bang, the *One* (God) individuated into fractals called OverSouls, or what I like to call our higher selves. Unlike on Earth, each OverSoul operates outside the laws of time and space and has its own individual refractions or avatars called Individual Soul Rays.

An individual Soul Ray is one life experience and occurs when form (our physical body) comes together with our split OverSoul; that is, the *soul-essence* we take with us into each life experience.

Each physical Earth life or experience is but a small part of the entire Individual Soul Ray life. The full experience includes what some call the pre-existence, the earth life experience, or other realities, as well as the post-life experience. The Individual Soul Ray is coherent with its OverSoul, the only difference being that the Individual Soul Ray is aligned with physical form and its own consciousness and identity. With each Individual Soul Ray acting as its own entity and its own governing body.

The form each Individual Soul Ray takes for their life experience, i.e. what they physically look like, goes beyond the 3D form of Earth and is why mediums and psychics are often able to see our loved ones as they looked when they were still alive. They typically connect to them in a dimension or reality that is part of their post-life experience, where they look as they did when alive on Earth.

This is why we hear people speak about loved ones or those who've passed as looking as they did when they were alive.

Form is always with its ISR consciousness, even when not seen in another dimension. For example, in the ISR post-life experience, souls are described as beings of light, who can zip and zoom anywhere they want, by thought alone. Though the human body is not seen here, it's still present and connected to the ISR consciousness.

In every life experience, each ISR, either consciously or unconsciously, has access to multiple other dimensions, levels, and realities. Ancient Egypt is a prime example of a culture that not only understood but was skilled and adept in consciously accessing other dimensions and realities. Whether through astral traveling, bilocation, quantum leaping, or tapping into various states of consciousness through deep meditative states. They did this, often leaving their physical body in a protected space while they travelled to these other places.

Skills Jesus was also taught how to do.

The Eqyptians were also skilled at healing through the use of the Zero Point Field and used this knowledge when constructing the Great Pyramids. These massive structures were built via specific geographical and astrological points and were important for raising the vibratory, healing and energy frequency of the area.

One of our ultimate goals, for spiritual advancement, is to advance in awareness and experience, enough to shift from a state of a singular perspective, or one life experience, to becoming adept and fully participating in the multidimensional world that we *all* live in.

We are all capable of attaining the *One Consciousness Evolution*, when we become aware of and start to work within the multiverse.

In order to attain the 'One Consciousness' we must learn and understand the Universal laws of the multiverse, functioning intelligently, responsibly, and ethically. And we must shift to an awareness where the Individual Soul Ray becomes conscious of all its multidimensional options.

Jesus did this in the Garden of Gethsemane and multiple other times throughout his life. He had a near-perfect understanding of how to tap into the Field, allowing him to commune with nature sprites in order to nourish and provide him with sustenance. At other times he endured multiple psychic attacks from entities that he had to command to leave. Most importantly, Jesus communed and spoke with God, preparing for his upcoming crucifixion. He was consciously aware of *all* his multidimensional options.

As divine souls, we are eternal, learning through each avatar experience and each ISR lifetime, offering multiple experiences for growth. One life we're the sick, hungry child whose spirit and death touched countless lives during the duration of their short life. In the next life, we experience what it's like as a rich prince, adding to the repertoire of our soul.

On Earth, when we incarnate, we forget the entirety of who we are, where we came from, and what we can do. We basically start from scratch in each and every life, regardless of who or what we've been in others. On rare occasions, our soul may remember all or parts of our true spiritual selves, but the majority of us forget.

These are the Earthly rules of existence; rules which don't necessarily apply to lives we experience from other realities and dimensions.

Ultimately, it is our soul's purpose is to remember this truth, that we are truly the Divine Self, through lifetimes of reincarnation, experience, and evolutionary soul growth. Through this process—the discovery of who we've been, what we've experienced, the wrongs we've committed, and the love and service we've given—these experiences become a part of who we are, and a guide for our current individual soul-ray life.

For example, one of my personal purposes in this ISR experience as Elisa is to remember who I've been, understand my inner power, and remember many of the lives I've lived, in order to guide my spiritual path.

Brian L Weiss describes this perfectly in his book *Many Lives, Many Masters*, where in past life hypnosis of a client, he learns that we're here to become "God-like through knowledge," and there is always choice. After each death, we transition to one of several planes of existence, depending on our level of progression, and subsequent vibratory frequency. A life led in service and kindness to others, learning to forgo the ego, and led with compassion, leads to a higher frequency and a greater conscious understanding and awareness. That life is filled with more love, compassion, harmony, and balance. In other words, a life filled with high-frequency emotions and thoughts.

A life of violence, greed, manipulation, and self-gratification is a life filled with lower-frequency emotions such as anger, self-doubt, fear, guilt, and shame; leading to a lower level of progression and need for serious life review and learning.

The idea that we must receive retribution for any sin we commit is less about God punishing us versus the punishment we inflict upon ourselves. Low-frequency emotions and thoughts are powerful enough to keep us trapped under their weight, especially after we die. When the guilt and shame of what we've done are seen with clarity, they can keep us stuck, and we often relive our nightmarish deeds over and over.

When we develop addictions, like alcohol and drugs, that aren't cleared in a present life, we carry them over to another. As we can only rid ourselves of bad habits in a 'physical state', such as the Earth life experience. Unfortunately, we're unable to clear those habits in our post-life experience or what many call the afterlife.When I was 22 years old, I had my wisdom teeth removed and was given Vicoprofen as my pain medication. I remember the first time I took it. I thoroughly enjoyed the warm, fuzzy feeling it created in my body, like something I'd felt before; a familiar friend you haven't seen in a while. It was a feeling I was drawn to experience over and over again and I knew after the first few days, that I couldn't keep the medication or those feelings. I knew this could become a problem.

Fast forward several years later when I learned I was Elizabeth Taylor, the legendary movie icon but also addicted to drugs and alcohol. My soul remembered those addictions.

In addition to habits, we accumulate and carry over certain abilities and play out contracts as well as Karmic debts with members of our soul family. And we agree to experience certain events, moments, and trauma.

All agreed to before incarnation of the avatar experience or the Individual Soul Ray life, in order to give us the experience our soul requires.

As it's only through our own inner healing, awareness, and spiritual evolution that we can and will attain the knowledge and expertise for personal salvation. Meaning that *we* create our own heaven or hell, not some powerful God who wants to punish us when we've made mistakes.

An example of this is when souls remain connected to the 3D frequency of the Earth, though their soul has left their physical body. We call them ghosts. Typically, when a person on Earth dies, their soul's frequency energetically transitions to a place where they'll undergo a full life review, a soul cleansing, and a remembering. Here our guides, members of our soul family, and others help us make sense of the life experience we had, find areas we could have made different choices, and help reconcile it all.

This happens whether a life was taken by suicide or the person died from natural causes at the age of 90.

But depending on the lifetime or experience, we don't always transition as we should and can get stuck.

I use my husband Brian's great-grandfather as an example. I never knew the man but heard that while alive, he'd committed several egregious acts and he wasn't the nicest person. In fact, at one point in time, he sued his own son and held him at gunpoint.

In July 2021, my family was at a Leadership Empowerment Retreat with several known gifted healers and psychics. My husband and I were using my parent's trailer for the week and my kids were sleeping in tents with their cousins on the property.

The retreat was held at a place called the Rapid Eye Institute in Salem, Oregon and every summer the owners host an 8-day gathering called 'Souls With Stamina' where healers, trainers, and many others come from all over come to participate and be a part of the retreat. For me, I get my soul fed. Aura pictures, sound healing, chakra realignments, tarot reads, mind-boggling stretches, fire walks, and in the last couple of years, I've been blessed to be a small group leader, my absolute favorite part.

That week I had my entire family, something I was beyond excited about. Emi was 11 going on 12 and was mostly hanging with Lisa, the niece of the Rapid Eye Founder and the main cook for the week. Lisa is also an incredibly gifted psychic, and she loves my girls, and they love her. I had asked her to give me a reading and finally, on the last day there we were sitting down to do it.

"I've been seeing a guy hanging around your family this week. He says he's Brian's Great Grandpa," Lisa told me.

She continued, "I think Emi has seen him too." Then she described him wearing same outfit Emi had described earlier. "He's asking for help, and he showed me what looks like images moving across a picture screen, a sequence of his life. He was raped as a small boy and abused often. And this man was gross, really mean, like not a good guy at all. He never left this realm because he's worried about his punishment. But now he says he's ready, and he's asking for help to leave."

"Of course," I said, "let's help him."

For the next several minutes we helped him get to where he needed to go for soul cleansing and healing. Lisa connected to God and with him, commanding in the name of God that his spirit was to be released. A process I've since learned, helping many others do the same. After a minute or two, he was gone.

The biggest takeaway here was that the things he did in his life as Brian's Grandfather, were dark and low frequency enough, that he wasn't able to transition in a normal manner due to his guilt, shame, and fear over what he had done to others, and who he had been. He'd created his own hell on Earth after dying, wandering around as a ghost with no real purpose and just existing with the vile actions he'd created for himself and others while he was alive. He lived in his own nightmare, over and over.

And while Lisa helped him go from this realm to wherever he needed to go, a definite step up, he will still have serious life reflection to do, and to make amends.

That process will most likely happen through karmic interactions with many of the same souls that he hurt but in a different avatar and ISR experience.

This is where Karma comes in. Karma is where the assaulted becomes the assaulter or the hunter the hunted. It's yet another opportunity for spiritual and evolutionary growth and to see and understand the yin and the yang, the binary world of complementary forces but often perceived as opposites.

Let's use another example of this process. Gabriel Fernandez was an 8-year-old boy who was brutally and horrifically beaten and tortured to death by his Mom and her boyfriend over a period of 8 months.

Why would God have allowed something so horrific to happen to a child? I often wonder this and at the same moment, I know that the importance of the experience, from a universal, multi-dimensional, and spiritual evolutionary perspective, is *far* bigger, deeper, and more important than we realize.

Gabriel's role and experience were far beyond the horrific impact that it had on him, or on his soul. It was necessary for tens if not hundreds of thousands of other people as well.

I firmly believe that prior to his birth, Gabriel contracted and agreed to undergo and experience what occurred to him. His soul agreed to go through it, both for his own evolutionary growth and karmic debts to repay but most importantly for the impact his experience would have on the world.

His horrific murder shocked and impacted agencies such as the Department of Children and Family Services.

Just as it impacted social and case workers the world over.

And it will have an impact on teachers, parents, caregivers, or other mandatory reporters when their gut screams that something is horribly wrong.

Without a doubt I know, the loss and brutal murder of Gabriel will save many children in similar circumstances.

Each and every life experience is what we need and agree to, contracting and coordinating with other souls, for spiritual evolution and to attain the highest understanding and awareness, that of a God.

I was recently told by Lisa I've had over 2200 lives, a higher number than most souls she has come across in her life. That means I've had experiences, a lot of experiences.

And part of those experiences was coming to know and understand the dark. This means that I've also been people in history who were cruel, unkind, and what most of us would term as evil.

I've done a lot...the yin and the yang, the light and the dark, that is often discussed in the Bible.

The Bible quotes Jesus as saying, "I am the way, and the truth, and the life. No one comes to the Father but through Me,"

Unfortunately, this famous passage was misinterpreted.

Jesus was really saying that all you must do, to reach spiritual attainment is to use him as an example, to watch what he's doing, and follow his lead. To reach spiritual mastery and attainment, we must gain experiences through multiple lifetimes, and we must let go of our baggage in each of those lifetimes. In addition, we must be willing to heal our generational and lifetime pain because *all* of us have and experience it. What isn't healed holds us back. And not being healed, often leads us to *dis-ease* such as depression, chronic pain, or even cancer.

Much of what Jesus was doing in the Garden of Gethsemane was not about taking on the sins of the world. He was releasing and clearing the generational and emotional pain and trauma for his line, and being a proxy for the world, for the entire collective at the same time.

As so many others have done before Jesus, and since his time, at different times in history.

Jesus's teachings were to awaken and show others how powerful these teachings are, that we each have healing abilities and spiritual gifts, and part of our purpose, in this 3D world, is to remember the truth of who we are and use each lifetime, each experience as a ladder rung on the climb to full spiritual attainment.

All while utilizing the power afforded to us through the use of the Zero Point Field.

The direct connection of healing energy straight to God which each of us has the ability to access and utilize.

We are the creators of our own destiny, and what we put out into the Universe—whether our conscious thoughts and emotions and/or unconscious thoughts and emotions—are what continue to create the world and worlds we experience throughout time.

Originally baptisms were not about "cleansing our sins" but were ritualistic ways to cleanse our auras, ground ourselves, call on our Guardian Angels, and to energetically place ourselves into our bubble of psychic protection. Extending 5 to 8 feet from our physical bodies, our auras are the ethereal and subtle energy system that is surrounding, within, and a part of each divine soul. Through our Chakras, it's our energetic connection to God. Guardian Angels on the other hand are powerful souls who work for God in the ethereal as well as our physical world. Though typically not seen, we're surrounded by our own team of Angels and Guides, sending us Universal messages through numbers, dreams, and synchronicities.As souls, we're in a continuous process of purging the negative energies, entities, and influences out of our auric fields. Years later, when I learned this truth, I was shocked and excited to learn I'd unknowingly been doing a similar practice.

For the past two or three years, my showers are often a sacred and ceremonious time and a very significant part of my spiritual practice. It started in February of 2020 when I began noticing inspirational thoughts and ideas about life, my future, and my dreams during my shower time. Soon I began receiving impressions of what I should do and/or when I should do something. Eventually, they became my number one meditation space and since then I've come to use my showers to fully connect, often using them for a breathwork journey, an 'I Am" meditation, or for a necessary energetic healing. These are tools that anyone can learn how to do and utilize for their own good.

Prior to showering, I sage or cleanse the space with *palo santo*, light my candles, and turn off the lights. When hot water permits, I commune for an hour or more with God, picturing the spray of the shower as pure Divine healing light washing over my body and aura. Many times, as I commune with God, I am also in contact with my sister, my guides, or my higher self. Other times I work on energetically clearing patterns or issues that are causing me angst. Sometimes I simply cry, leaning into and feeling what's coming up.

This is a practice I'm truly grateful for and feel certain that both Princess Diana and Elizabeth Taylor enjoyed their shower or bath time as a tranquil and necessary reprieve as well.

By the end of Alchemy, I saw, felt, knew, and believed these were the main differences between how much of the world felt about Jesus and how I believed Him actually to be.

And ever since then, maybe a dozen times since, when someone has asked how I see myself when I close my eyes, the same image of Jesus comes to mind.

Chapter Three

When Alchemy was over, I started focusing on my future.

For the past 8 - 9 years, I'd spent approximately 60 to 80 hours a week learning the art of what most call traditional or Western medicine; first as a medical student, then as a medical resident and physician in training. By the time I finished my residency in June of 2013, I was beyond excited to start building my dreams.

I began my private practice career as a family medicine physician and obstetrician in a Women's Healthcare and Reproductive Clinic in Ontario, Oregon. Most of my practice was obstetrics (OB), with over 60% of them pregnant Moms. The other 40% were primarily teenagers and women, with only a few men.

Coming out of residency, I was carrying over $400,000 in student loans and found myself pulling out of my contract with the hospital. I was supposed to work for St. Alphonsus in the same clinic as my dad. However, for some reason, they decided that as an employee, I wouldn't be able to work with him, which was my entire reason for coming to Ontario in the first place. We didn't necessarily want to be in Ontario, but they offered us $100,000 in residency, a Godsend. I was willing to settle, with the promise to work with my dad and have a guaranteed job and financial stability when I graduated.

Add the additional $100,000 I owed to the hospital to pay them back, while incurring clinic and office expenses, and my financial state was quickly over my head. And with the promise to my girls, particularly Taylor, that they'd have every opportunity for dance, we spent insane amounts of time, energy, gas, and money hauling them 45 minutes to dance class one way; four, five, and sometimes six days a week.

I was in a vortex and didn't know how to escape it. After two years of difficulties in making a living as a private practice physician, working in an OB Gyn office, and seeing the future financial devastation coming down the pipes when we lost another physician from the group, Brian and I finally decided to see what other opportunities were out there.

Barely looking, I stumbled upon two job openings near or in Bend, Oregon. One was working for St. Charles, the biggest healthcare system in Central Oregon. I'd initially forgotten that I had interviewed with them a year prior but hadn't pursued that job as I'd decided to give another big push to make Ontario work. This time around, I decided to do an in-person, on-site interview for both jobs during the same visit.

I was offered $180,000 for the job within Bend proper and $220,000 for the job in Redmond. I took the job in Redmond even though we knew my monthly income was insufficient to pay our monthly bills. I made approximately $12,000 net monthly. Our rent was $2200, my student loans were approximately $2500 or more per month, I was paying $2000+/monthly to pay back the money borrowed in residency and for office start-up costs, plus we paid approximately $2000 per month for the girls' school tuition (because I was adamant they not get sucked into public school education which I felt was oppressive and lacked to inspire creative adults with critical thinking skills).

I wanted my girls to have the world, the best, to have it all. And this included dance at anywhere from $15,000 - $20,000/year as it was the *only* activity Taylor wanted to do. The end result being we were often short each month.

At the same time, we had some breathing room as I was still receiving obstetrical and other insurance reimbursements that take months to come in. We had more than 6 months reserve with the plan that this would give my husband's new house-flipping business a chance to get on its feet and start making a return.

Unfortunately, the return never came, and eventually, our money reserve ran out. When I realized there was no guarantee of when Brian's company would turn itself around, I began looking for a moonlighting job that I started January of 2018. I found it through the Oregon Women's Physician Group on Facebook, where one of the members directed me to a small hospital in Burns, OR, called Harney District. They were looking for physicians to cover the weekends, from 6:00 PM Friday evening until 6:00 AM Monday morning, a 60-hour shift consisting of both ER and inpatient care. The weekends were supposedly a crap shoot in terms of busyness, but I was told I brought the shit-storm with me. Nine times out of ten, I'd barely sleep during my shifts. Occasionally, depending on the severity of the weekend, I'd give myself a reprieve and call sick into work at St. Charles on Monday. But mostly, I kept going; I'd suck it up, shower, pack, and leave Burns by 6 am to arrive at Redmond in time to see my first patient by 8:30 AM or 9:00 AM. By 6:00 PM Monday night, I'd have worked 72 straight hours, often with only a handful of hours of sleep.

But each shift brought another $7,000 into our account and kept us going.

I worked a shift every 4 to 6 weeks until March 2020, often combining them with vacation and/or while I was coming and going. Sometimes I'd work two weekends in a row and/or begin adding shifts during the week if I had availability. While I loved and enjoyed the staff and those I worked with, I didn't enjoy the work. I was tired, exhausted, and burning out.

When I was home, I had no energy for anything else. I felt compelled to write but had no energy for writing. I felt compelled to teach others but had no wherewithal or knowledge of how to make that happen. Most of all, what little or extra money we had was spent on the girls, their dance, and their summer activities, which typically all revolved around dance. They'd spend weeks and months traveling from Texas to Vegas or California, taking dance intensives. I was more than happy to do it because they loved it, and I loved providing it to them.

But, in choosing to spend our money the way we did, there was no extra time, money, or vacation to spend on me, my healing, or my dreams of becoming a speaker and building my skills in energy work. I slowly started to feel myself sinking further inward and becoming more resentful and stuck.

My health also took a hit. Too many hours worked, too many interrupted nights, and most importantly, I wasn't using my voice in the way I felt compelled. I didn't believe in the medical model in the way they wanted me to practice. We are encouraged to over-use medications, spend too little time with our patients, refuse to look at poly-pharmacy's impact on a grand level, and not ask enough questions about guidelines. Instead, they prefer we act like robots. Most importantly, we spend too little time on emotional and mind/body health. We try to mask mental and emotional health with a pill, an anti-depressant, anti-psychotic, or anti-anxiolytic when the truth is that when we suppress those emotions, they lodge in the body and, over time, can and do create dis-*ease*.

Worst of all, the bulk of the medical industry is saturated in corruption, greed, and the need for control. Pharmaceutical companies cherry-pick study results to get their drug approved while overlooking stats, length of study time, number of participants, or countless other red flags regarding a medication. All while up-charging their medications by 500% to 1000+% or more, making it *very* difficult for some to buy their life-saving medications. For example, a month's worth of insulin is typically over $1000/month while costing the pharmaceutical companies pennies to make.

The emotional impact for me was I felt out of dissonance in what I was doing for my patients versus what I should have been doing for them, helping them heal their emotional pain (whether manifesting as a mental health disorder, autoimmune disease, or chronic pain such as fibromyalgia). Instead, I was part of the continued problem, masking them with medications.

More importantly, I felt called to be of service in a different way other than working in a clinic and seeing patients one on one.

I was the best eater there was, paleo through and through. I hardly ever wavered, except for alcohol. And I was an avid Cross-fitter and loved to exercise. But something happened shortly after we moved to Bend. My ability to do what I used to do in Cross-fit changed drastically. I felt more tired and fatigued; my muscles ached more, I was slower, and I couldn't move as fast. I felt like I was moving through water or mud, and my thinking was slower. Not as quick as it used to be.

While I used to finish my Workout of the Day (WOD) in the top 15% to 20% of people, I could now barely finish my WODs at all.

At the time, I remember consciously choosing to stay at St. Charles and to forgo writing a book or work to become a spiritual influencer. I had a family to feed and would get the opportunity when Brian's business took off.

Then one day, at the end of January 2016, I injured my left lower gluteal and lumbar area while lifting light deadlifts, causing months of neuropathy, foot drop, and excruciating pain.

If the injury wasn't bad enough, I'd been gaining weight and dealing with constipation, hair loss, and cyclic changes. The physical impact of not using my voice, of not speaking my truth, resulted in my thyroid becoming underactive. Adding insult to injury, my beautiful and younger-than-me sister passed away in May of 2017 from complications due to breast cancer. She was only 36 years old, leaving behind two beautiful boys.

Her death, under normal circumstances of a sister losing a sister, was devastating for me and my family. However, I, in particular, took it very hard. Unable to take the time I needed to properly mourn, I returned to work 1 week after her death and kept going.

I felt even more lost, stuck, and hopeless.

My daughter, as will be told in a later chapter, had a completely different experience of my sister's passing, the lasting effects of which would seep like tar into the lives of our family for the next 5 years.

But I kept going. Because one day, I told myself, it will all change, the money will be there, and I'll be able to do what I've always wanted.

Around this time, Brian decided to let his real estate business go, as it wasn't producing much if any return. He was an entrepreneur at heart and never wanted to work for anyone but himself. His dream to become a self-made millionaire by age 50 started when he was just a little boy and weaved its way through multiple start-up companies, investments, partnerships, and patent opportunities. He was beautifully and painfully optimistic, always seeing himself as a business leader, owner/investor of multi-million-dollar inventions, and huge entrepreneur of taking risks and possibilities. Over the years, we'd unknowingly invested in Ponzi schemes, new tech energy devices, high-risk real estate, and other companies that always promised a hefty return and big opportunities. He'd often turn to family members or friends as investors and partners.

Unfortunately, time after time, each investment, every million-dollar idea, saw its way to the end.

Over the years, we've invested $100,000+ in inventions such as Ax Sliders or a device, if it worked, that created free energy.

In 2008, we invested close to $125,000 in a townhouse development where the loan to finish the project was set to close the following Monday. But the following Monday, the market crashed. It was October 2008 and the start of losing everything financially. Just 2 months prior, Brian had compiled our net worth. At the time, we had almost 20 rental properties in the Boise, ID area. Most of them were rented, paying for themselves, and the Boise market, in particular, was in a very small bubble of opportunity. Most of the properties had jumped, in worth, by leaps and bounds, and for the first time, our net worth was right around $1,000,000. Brian had done it...his dream was coming true.

When the market crashed, we could no longer get a loan to finish the townhouse project. And when it crashed, the rental market crashed too. Then, for the first time, we had a mass exodus of renters who stopped paying and/or left their rental properties altogether. I was in medical school and receiving no income, and any income Brian had hoped to make in real estate came to a crashing halt. We could not handle the extra cost in payments, and slowly, one by one, our financial reserve fell away, and with it, our credit scores. Most of the houses ended up on short-sale lists, and eventually, we had nothing left.

After working several months for ATSU as an enrollment counselor (making 1/8 of what he'd been making in real estate), Brian returned to school to obtain his master's in project management.

In 2012 we invested $25,000+ (an inheritance he received from his Grandfather) into a company he started called Global Business Funding with a neighboring friend. This lasted a little over a year, took immense time and effort, and gave little to no return. We also invested another $5,000 into Blue Phoenix, another company that has yet to succeed.

And we were convinced by my sister-in-law to invest in a company promising another huge return. We didn't jump right into this one. Instead, we waited 2 or 3 months to see if she'd continue to be successful. When she was, we invested $5000 and convinced our good friends to invest $1000. The next day, it was halted for being a Ponzi scheme. We lost *all* our money, and we lost an additional $1000 because I felt so much guilt that we once again asked our friends to invest in something that went to shit, I worked an extra moonlighting shift and paid their $1000 back. These same friends had also invested $50,000 in the Ax slider invention and lost money there too.

By the time we moved back to the Boise area in 2013, Global Business Funding was no longer. The inventions were not happening, so for the next several years, Brian worked and helped with my family's worm castings business and started a new real estate business that he worked on with my brother Rob. In addition, he was our primary child caregiver, Brian filling in my missing gaps in parenting. The quintessential father, he has been involved in their lives since day one. Whether for child care, diaper changes, bus driver, bath song creator, or homework helper, he was there running the girls to and from most of their activities, school functions, and play dates. As a father and husband, he tops the charts, always doing whatever he can to make our lives easier.

His businesses may have occasionally made several thousand here or there, but overall, very little money came from the real estate investments. Eventually, he saw the futility and let it go.

In 2017 Brian formed a hemp business and partnership called Freedom CBD. By this time, our reserves were tapped, and we had no money to invest, but as he was an owner, he also didn't bring in much, if any, money.

And I kept working.

Always with the promise that as soon as Brian made it happen and made money, I could quit my job and finally do what I was passionate about; helping others heal their emotional and generational trauma.

The days turned into weeks, the weeks into months, and the months turned into years. In May of 2019, I found myself the heaviest (190 lbs), most depressed, and most unhappy I'd ever been in my life. I'm a Scorpio, and true to form, I've always loved feeling and being "sexy." And I've always enjoyed sex. But I honestly couldn't remember the last time my husband and I had sex. It had been at least 6 months, maybe longer. Not only had it been forever, but I lacked any sexual desire, and I was barely 40. Life felt mundane and purposeless, and I was simply living in a hamster wheel of existence.

I dreaded the daily work grind, couldn't wait for the weekend, and became terribly unhappy by Saturday night/Sunday morning as I knew Monday and work were just around the corner. I dreaded my day-to-day. I wasn't helping my patients to the fullest extent, nor was I healing myself.

I was miserable.

It's no wonder the Universe knew it needed to shake things up a bit and get me out of the monotony. It happened late in the afternoon at work in May of 2019. I had an opening and a patient from another provider's panel needed to see me for an acute sick visit for a large abscess that needed draining. I've drained hundreds of abscesses, big and small. They come in all shapes, sizes, and locations, and typically, when they're fluctuant, are easy to drain. His was very fluctuant and should have been very easy, so I'm still uncertain how I somehow stuck myself with the same scalpel I'd stuck him with moments earlier. And it just so happened he was HIV+.

Wanting to take all precautions and knowing the incredible anti-viral and anti-inflammatory effects of a high-quality CBD/THC oil, I began taking daily doses.

And over the next few weeks, my worldview changed.

Approximately two to three weeks later, I noticed I was laughing more, had less pain, was less serious, was sleeping better, and felt less closed off. In addition, I was starting to experience and feel sexual desire again.

In August of 2019, after a particularly rough day and a few difficult weeks financially, Brian looked at me and asked that I go with him somewhere. I said yes. We jumped in the car, and he drove to a dispensary where we purchased our first bit of weed in over 20 years.

After, we drove to the woods and smoked a joint together. I hadn't smoked since I was 20 years old, and Brian hadn't since he quit drinking alcohol 25+ years earlier and became sober in 1994. Suddenly, we were laughing together, looking at each other, and connecting again, something we hadn't done in what seemed like forever. It was a new start to seeing and discovering each other again. In some ways, I view this moment as a pivotal trajectory for our relationship. I'm not certain we'd be together today if it hadn't occurred. This moment opened enough of our hearts and broke down enough walls to allow some honest communication and a willingness to start anew.

The next few months at work were particularly stressful as St. Charles was changing the physician contract to one that dropped the compensation by $12,000/year, which could be made up in bonuses we could get from meaningful use and preventative measures. This meant that we'd be able to make our regular salary if, and only if, we had a certain percentage of our patients who took all their recommended vaccinations, had all their recommended screening tests, and followed all recommended prevention practices. Unfortunately, not all patients believe they need every recommended vaccination or preventative measure. In essence, we'd be "encouraging" patients to get them, in order to be paid, a huge conflict of interest and one completely against my moral and ethical code. I didn't want to be a part of this. For months I struggled with what I should do, but when the decision had to be made, I couldn't go against my morals simply for a pay check. I had to quit.

On the same day, I decided to quit, inspectors found black mold in the house we'd lived the longest. We would have to move, and we'd have to move quickly.

In one week, we'd found another property, packed all our stuff, and moved into the place where we'd live for the next 12 months. Several times during this period, I felt that the Universe was moving me in a particular direction, and I'd remark to myself about this very thing. It was also about this time I began seeing repeated numbers, multiples of 1's, 2's and 4's, 3's, 5's, 8's, or occasional 7's. I began noticing them on license plate numbers and signs everywhere I went.

As the months and years have passed, I now see triples and quadruples every day, and it's often not uncommon to see groupings of numbers in a row. Such as a 333's on a license plate followed by 333's immediately seen somewhere else; signs which I've realized are the Universe's way of communicating with me in its Universal language.

My job was set to end December 31^{st,} and I planned to continue with Burns and work a 6-month locums job on the coast of Oregon, starting in February. In January 2020, I began doing soul-searching and inner work on myself. While working on the coast, the plan was to get a DPC (Direct Primary Care) business up and going back to Bend. One of the biggest issues in medicine I saw was the corrupt insurance companies, and I wanted nothing to do with them. I was planning to build a business that would allow me to take the time needed to care for my patients the right way, one that would integrate traditional medicine with energy medicine, marrying the two in perfect harmony forming the *New* medicine.

In addition, my relationship with my oldest daughter Taylor had been difficult for a few years. And everything I was doing to try and get through to her wasn't working. Unable to reach her, I knew any work I did for myself would benefit her too. I paid for sessions with a well-known energy healer in our healing community, who did most of her sessions over the phone. She was very effective in clearing negative energy or stuck emotion and is also a very gifted intuitive. I worked with her when I had the left-sided neuropathy and foot drop. In a one-hour session, I went from being unable to stand for more than 30 seconds, due to intense pain, to being able to stand for more than an hour at a time. In my world, at that instance, she had just worked a miracle in my life.

During my sessions with her, I was told I had a bigger mission here than I could possibly fathom. Bigger than a DPC clinic in Bend. Had I not recently paid for psychic and numerology readings, both of which said the same thing, I probably wouldn't have believed her.

Based on my birthday and astrological chart, both readings claimed my mission and purpose would impact and affect the entire world. That I would become a celebrity of sorts, might even do some acting, and I'd have at least one daughter who would continue my life work with me. I was a speaker, a healer, and a humanitarian. I was also told that for approximately 3 months upcoming, I'd be afforded more insight, possibilities, spiritual connection, and spiritual awareness. Later, I'd be told the period was a time of heightened energy and expedited healing. According to my numerology charts, it would start at the end of March and last through the end of June or the beginning of July.

As my start time for the locums work on the coast came closer, I began having more angst and anxiety about going there. For all intents and purposes, I was the definition of a "burned-out" physician. A term I dislike using as it implies the onus is somehow on the physician themselves versus the deplorable working conditions most of us work in. I realize now it's easier for the hospitals and medical programs to feel good about how much they expect from their physicians when they put together "Physician Burnout" programs and Wellness classes. Their classes are laid out talking about and encouraging mindfulness, self-care, and exercise (where we're lacking and falling short) instead of discussing and talking about the ridiculous work hours, work requirements, paperwork expectations, 7:00 AM meetings, toxic work environments, or multiple other demands on our time, that interfere with our ability to self-care. Therefore, the blame rests on our shoulders to make sure we get up at the crack of 5:00 AM and complete our workout. Ignore the fact that we delivered a baby at 12:00 AM or rounded on our last patient at 9 pm last night. If we only took the time to do "x, y, and z," the burnout wouldn't exist.

But regardless of what you call it, I was emotionally tapped and physically spent from working in a clinic job that was neither fulfilling for myself nor fully effective for my patients. For the sake of "keeping money on the table" (a *very* high priority), I was returning to the exact job I despised.

Before quitting St. Charles, I had studied and/or worked approximately 50 to 80 hours/week for almost 15 years straight. Minus a week to a few weeks, here and there, I'd have off between transition, moving across the country, or starting a new job. When my family first moved to Bend in 2015, St. Charles didn't have me credentialed until late October. Not wanting the girls to start a new school mid-way through the year and not wanting to miss out on income potential, I stayed in Ontario for over 2 months while my family lived in Bend without me. My last day in Ontario was on a Monday, and my first day at St. Charles was the very next day on Tuesday.

But as the time neared for me to move to the coast and start my new job, the angst continued, and I didn't feel I was supposed to go. In my session later that day, Elayne confirmed what I'd been thinking; if I were to go to the coast and do the job, I wouldn't have the energy or time needed to get a clinic started, nor would I have the energy/time to fulfill the purpose I'd been hearing about from all my readings. If I wanted to fulfill my purpose, I'd have to jump and let the Universe know I was serious. Moreover, for the last 18 months, I'd had left-sided "digging" chest pain connected to tight muscles in my neck, chest, and scapular area. Every time I worked, I'd get a huge flare. Following every Burn's weekend, it would take two to three days to get everything to calm down. The area was constantly in pain, making my typing job more difficult. I knew if I started the job, the shoulder/scapular/neck pain would only get worse.

So, I turned the it down and increased the number of shifts I did in Burns. This way, I'd have more downtime to allow my body to heal.

Little did I know.

Chapter Four

At the beginning of February 2020, I drove to Ontario to help my Mom for a couple of days following a bilateral knee replacement. While there, I told her what I'd been told. "Mom, I don't know what it is, but there's something big I'm supposed to do. It's really big," I said.

"I see it similar to Deepak Chopra, but bigger," she replied. "And I'm feeling impressed to tell you to watch this episode on Gaia."

She was referring to an episode in one of Gregg Braden's series. In it, he specifically talked about heart-brain coherence and the importance of this in our day-to-day lives. Not only was the episode exactly what I needed to see, it also sparked my scientific mind. I began actively watching anything and everything related to the quantum field, Universal law, and quantum physics and I started watching everything Gregg Braden, Bruce Lipton, Joe Dispenza, and others. Similar to when I first watched '*The Secret*', it was information I intuitively resonated with and "knew," but at the same time, the science behind the information fascinated me the most.

At the end of February, I spent a particularly long, difficult, and exhausting weekend in Burns. Returning home, I jumped into the shower, sobbing and releasing the weekend, feeling the strong urge to quit my job at Burns. What followed were several minutes of intense conversations I had with God about why that wasn't possible. I had already agreed to take those shifts; it wouldn't be fair to back out now. I have to be responsible and take care of my family; if I quit this job, I'll have no guaranteed income.

All I felt was I needed to trust, the answer coming in the form of a deep twist to the gut, followed by an immediate knowing. One of the many ways in which God communicates with me.

Regardless, the Universe wasn't waiting to let me decide. Instead, it decided for me.

One week later, I was sitting cross-legged on a hotel room bed doing Bella's hair and makeup for a dance competition we were attending in Portland, OR.

Going to stand, my left knee suddenly felt painfully tight and stuck, unable to release or loosen, and instantly swelled to double the size. And when I placed my foot on the ground, sharp pains shot up into the knee area and upper quads. I could barely walk, and my knee was twice the size in minutes.

There was no way I could work effectively; especially with the pain of my shoulder, neck, and scapular area worsening, added to the mix.

Because of this, I had to cancel the rest of my shifts.

We had no idea how to survive financially, but I did my best to trust the process.

At the end of March, Covid officially came to the States, and we went into lockdown, something my soul was craving; reprieve and connection.

By the end of March, I rated my shoulder/neck pain an 8/10 most days and my knee the same. I hobbled everywhere, couldn't put full weight on my left leg, and could barely type or work on the computer without immense (burrowing) pain in my chest area. Not realizing sitting could cause such a severe injury, and due to the pandemic, we couldn't get easy imaging, my official diagnosis was missed for several months.

Had I gotten it right after the injury, my surgery would have been emergent, in hopes that the lateral meniscus flap caught in the middle of my knee could've been saved.

Regardless, I remember knowing and feeling, on a deep soul level, the yearning I felt for reprieve. And when lockdown happened, I went within.

We were living in Bend, OR, and had just moved into the house the prior November when the black mold was discovered. I mentioned feeling the Universe pulling us along at times, this house being one such example.

It was like the Universe knew our family would need the space, in the house, for when the pandemic hit, and I needed the beautiful forest 1.5 blocks down the road. We could barely afford it, but the house provided the perfect sanctuary for our family. Interestingly and unbeknownst at the time of renting, we were only two blocks from my sister Becky. The Universe was most definitely guiding us.

Listening to my intuition that this time was for me to go inward, I consciously chose to get off all social media and didn't watch the news for almost two months.

While I wasn't sure what the virus was exactly, I knew that what the news was relaying didn't feel right either. And I didn't agree with how it was being handled.

By pushing the fear.

Fear creates more fear. Beyond, it's one of the lowest-frequency emotions we can exhibit and one of the most damaging. Not only did the lockdown keep people away from their loved ones, bringing high-frequency emotions such as love, but it also kept many in the low frequency of fear. Creating more disease.

Multiple centers and integrative healing practices utilize, treat, and understand emotions' direct impact on our overall health. Not only does every emotion have its own frequency (please see the graph Hawkin's Scale of Consciousness), but emotions literally create our future reality.

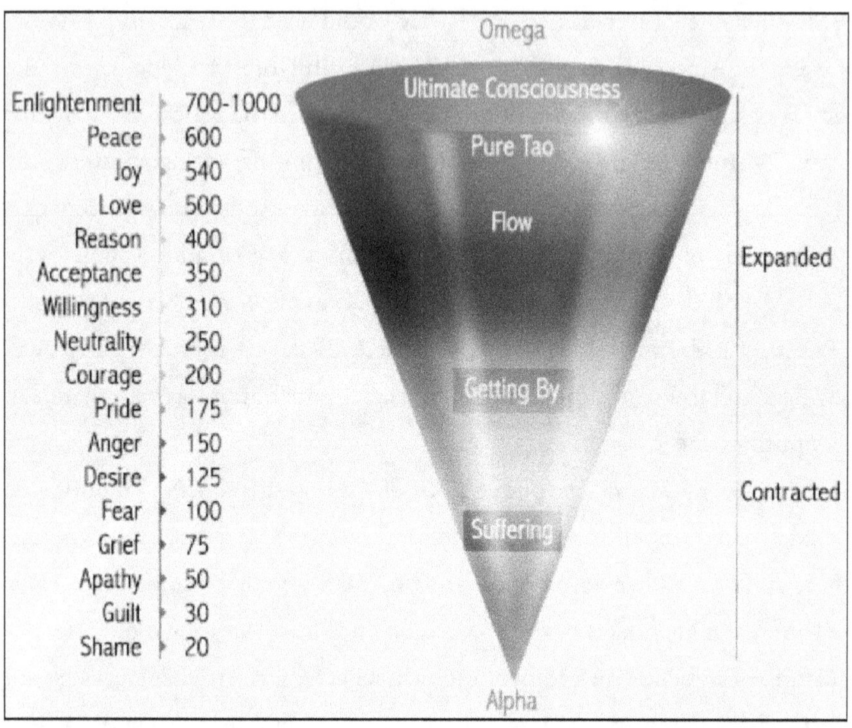

It's Universal law.

Any time we feel any emotion, it first registers in the limbic area of our brain, creating a cascade response and sending signals to every cell in the body to create more of that same feeling and emotion. When we feel joy, peace, love, clarity, or other high frequency emotions, the vibratory signals sent from the limbic system are also high frequency. When this occurs our DNA begins to open and unwind in to creation, expansiveness and growth.

By contrast when our body feels fear, and other low frequency emotions, our bodies contract, meaning we shut down, restrict, and stop all forward movement.

Think about what happens to your body when you feel afraid. How does your stomach feel? What happens to your thoughts? Does your heart race? Do your palms become sweaty?

This is necessary in times of fight or flight, as it spurs us into our best course of action.

But what happens when the feeling of fear is all around us, surrounding us, inundating us?   Not just when it spurs us into immediate action on occasion, but feels like a punch in the gut most of the time?

Multiple scientific studies show what physiologically happens to our body when we're consistently sitting in and/or being inundated with a low-frequency emotion, such as fear.

In the 1990s, a microbiologist by the name of Bruce Tainio developed a machine which measured certain frequencies emanating from the body. With it, he found a specific frequency that depending on the level predicted one's ability to become sick, catch a virus, acquire cancer, or those able to supersede illnesses. When the person's frequency stayed above 62 Hz, they were healthy, with no illnesses. Having a frequency below 60 Hz increased one's risk for viruses and colds, and below 58 Hz increased one's risk for any and all diseases. At a consistent frequency of 42 Hz, cancer was able to develop in the body and he also found that when someone smoked a cigarette, their frequency would drop to 42 Hz.

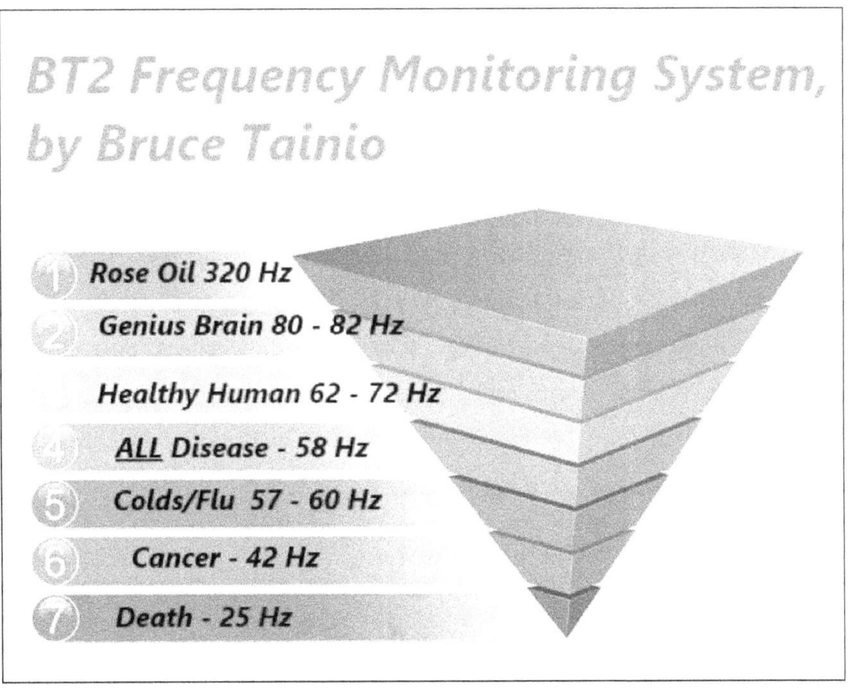

Bruce also found that death in the body starts around 25 Hz. Though I haven't found what instrument was used, everything I find about fear shows it measuring around 19 Hz, below the level at which death begins in the body.

Fear paralyzes us to the point of stopping body systems from working effectively or working at all.

It actually stops the unwinding of our DNA and creates free radicals, toxic debris, and the inability to be in balance and harmony.

For the last 25 years, the Heart/Math Institute has been studying the effects of our emotions on the heart. They've shown low-frequency emotions, like fear, cause an erratic and poor heart rate variability or HRV, the heart-brain-nervous system interaction agent. And what they've shown, over the years, is that a poor or low HRV is associated with most chronic diseases; the biggest being heart problems, dementia, and autoimmune diseases.

By contrast, regular and consistent feelings of joy, happiness, or peace result in a more balanced, harmonious HRV, adding to one's emotional resilience and significantly decreasing one's risk of developing dis-Ease.

High-frequency emotions raise our overall frequency, keeping us healthier and less likely to become sick.

I use the Hawkins Scale of Consciousness as an easy tool to discuss and talk about the importance of our emotions with my patients and clients. As you can see via the picture, being in the flow (another term for heart-brain coherence) begins around 400, along with emotions such as acceptance and reason. It isn't until 500 or higher that we can step into the higher frequency emotions such as love, peace, and joy, bringing us more clarity and expansiveness.

For more information on the importance of our emotions, thoughts, and learned behaviors, you can watch my Quantal U video series at:www.4bodhi.com/about-quantal-u/.

In terms of the pandemic, everything about the virus was fear. Fear porn everywhere, regardless of what side you believe. It was either the virus will kill us all, so you'd better stay inside, wear a mask (even if exercising), and don't see your family or loved ones, or you may be responsible for killing them.

FEAR! Versus...

The virus is a lie; they're lying to us. It's the elite trying to depopulate the World. They want us sick and reliant on them.

FEAR!

Everywhere. Throughout. Causing more fear and illness.

I was determined not to get sucked in and instead stayed away from all social media and news reports.

Bend is typically cold and snowy in April, but not this spring. Most days the weather was 40 to 60 degrees, sunny and beautiful. I'd take my phone, set of headphones, blanket, and water and go into the woods, where I found a specific spot looking out over the mountains. There I'd place my blanket down, lay on my back, and work to connect to the Earth and myself.

Here I learned to truly meditate for the first time in my life. Sometimes I'd spend 2-4 hours out there working on it.

Not knowing how to properly meditate and finding it difficult to keep my thoughts from interfering, I started with guided meditations found on YouTube. From there I began using binaural beats to help me focus and I discovered the healing benefit of utilizing breathing and deep vibrational sounds during my meditations.

I found that my pain was better when I could get to a place of nothingness or beingness, and I didn't hurt as intensely. Overall I felt better, my attitude was improved, and I had a better sense of purpose and living.

My kids and husband remarked on and felt it too. They described me as calmer, patient, and less serious or high-strung. It was noticeably different.

And then one day in late April, while meditating, my neck, shoulder, scapular and knee pain seemed to slip away, though my knee was still swollen, and I walked with a severe limp. When I opened my eyes, everything looked different, brighter, more beautiful. I felt love for *everything!* I was in a heightened state of consciousness that, while it dimmed over time, lasted several days longer. I felt magnificent and ready to tackle the World. The only problem was I didn't know what that would be or how it would look.

Suddenly I had no idea what I was supposed to do. In my sessions with Elayne, we talked about needing a website, and I felt I'd somehow be on TV or in front of people. I'd often daydream about being on stage, in front of large audiences, and teaching others how to heal. Heal from deeply rooted issues, keeping them stuck, unable to progress. At a psychic party I hosted, when I was still planning to open a Direct Primary Care (DPC) practice (where patients pay a monthly fee to secure my services vs using insurance) in January of 2020, the psychic told me I'd be cutting my hair (which I hadn't done yet nor thought I would ever do), that I'd be in front of people, and would be very successful. A week earlier, I attended a Christmas party and told a group of women I'd been feeling similar energy as JoAn of Arc and was feeling my "warrior Goddess emerging." An hour later, my tarot card was pulled, and it was the Warrior Goddess card remarking on the same energy that Joan of Arc tapped into when she was alive and leading an army of men.

The buzz of change was in the air, and I felt it too. Now what exactly did God want me to do?

Feeling stuck, I called my Mom, and she recommended I do a session with a gifted Tibetan Bowl practitioner and with Lynell, a gifted psychic and founder's daughter of an integrative therapy called Rapid Eye Technology (RET).

Similar to EMDR (eye movement desensitization therapy), rapid eye technology is an energy modality that recreates the same eye movements we go through when asleep in the theta state of consciousness. During this state we're most able to process, release and reconcile the day through specific eye movements relating to our traumatic memories, our physical self, emotional self, and our mental and spiritual self. Created by a Mom looking to help her autistic son in the 1960's, RET has now grown world wide and is helping people everywhere.

Tibetan bowl therapy, on the other hand, uses the sound, tones and vibrations made by the bowls, to clear blocked frequencies from our auric fields that are causing problems and disease.

After our session, the Tibetan practitioner advised me to undergo an intense EMF (electromagnetic force) cleanse: laying in a bath filled with baking soda and celtic sea salt, fully submerged, and using a snorkel apparatus to breathe. Produced by microwaves, electric poles, and most electronics, EMFs are notoriously known for bogging down and interfering with our energy bodies, blocking meridians; and often causing mental fatigue, brain fog, and an inability to get clear answers from our inner knowing.

From God.

Symptoms of EMF exposure often include skin tingling, erythema, and burning sensations; as well as neurological side effects such as fatigue, light-headedness, heart palpitations, digestive issues, and difficulty concentrating.

To help me clear the effects of EMF, I was to lay in this bath for 15 minutes. He also told me to suit up; the next several months would be intense.

I drove to Salem, OR, and spent six hours with Lynell, clearing archetypes, releasing trauma, and letting go of things I'd held onto, things not serving me in the best way anymore. When leaving, I watched Lynell light up when I mentioned the word *biofield*. There was something about that word.

The human biofield is defined as the extension of our subtle energy systems intricately interwoven throughout our physical and biological bodies. In addition, it surrounds and extends approximately 6-8 feet beyond our physical form and is our connection with all other matter.

In that moment, I felt certain much of my future work, would center around this.

I was emotionally and energetically drained when I left her place, but I felt immensely freer and lighter.

The next morning I was sitting on the couch when suddenly, like an electric zap, I had a download of what I was to do. Develop videos that teach about the energy aspect of ourselves, the importance of meditation, and our emotions and thoughts regarding our health. In addition, I felt people needed to know about the incredible and amazing integrative therapies that get to the root cause of healing. Through my website, I wanted to create a smorgasbord of information about various healers, therapies, and how to access them, giving people a comprehensive team for healing.

I immediately thought of my friend Hector, whom I met in med school and who has similar views to mine on spirituality and the Universe. When I called and asked if he wanted to visit and help create my videos, he immediately said yes. It was the beginning of May, and Hector planned to arrive at the beginning of June.

The next 4 weeks were a blur as I had 4 episodes to write before Hector arrived. He planned to spend several weeks with us, even attending a self-empowerment course called Souls With Stamina, an 8-day course that pushes you out of your comfort zone and opens new levels of consciousness, ideas, and awareness. It also teaches group compatibility, including multiple work connections and opportunities we hoped to have.

SWS was the last week of June that summer, and I had never been but had always wanted to go. Several years prior, I sent my then 12-year-old daughter Taylor, to attend with my Mom. I came up for one day to see her and participate in a fire walk, vowing to return.

On the first day, I was a bundle of energy and excitement; at the end of the day, we met in our small groups for the first time. Hector and several others were there, and our group leader was Deb Spendlove. Deb was the perfect group leader. Psychic and intuitively connected, she's full of emotions, insights, and intuitive hits, and she doesn't hesitate to let you know. She suffered horrendous abuse as a child and is happy to share her experience for teaching purposes. She was and is a beautiful example of not letting the past get in the way of her future.

We were each asked to tell a little about ourselves, and when it was my turn, I said, "My name is Elisa Peavey. Many of you know my Mom, Eileen, who is here also. I'm a family practice physician. I've felt impressed to create a business, letting people know about different healing practices, such as Rapid Eye and others, that I feel are important for full energetic, spiritual, and emotional healing. I'm excited to be here, learn more, and get to know more about myself."

When I finished, Deb simply looked at me and said, "Elisa, do you know you have grief all over your field?"

With that, I dropped to the ground and started balling.

And it didn't stop. I cried all night, minus a couple of hours' worth of pitiful sleep. When I woke alone in my tent at 3-4 in the morning, I started crying and sobbing again. I couldn't get it to stop; it was uncontrollable.

While I cried, I thought of my sister. I was beyond sad she was gone, and I couldn't help her. And yet, at the same time, I had a very distinct feeling that she agreed to go when she did and contracted to leave when she did. Part of this contract was so she could assist our mission from the other side.

Regardless, the tears wouldn't stop, and finally, at 7:00 AM I texted Deb: "I need help. I can't stop crying. Can you please come?"

She quickly came to my tent and using her Rapid Eye wand and Immediate Release Technique (IRT), helped me calm and damn the crying...for the time being.

Two hours later, I pulled myself to class, complete with the puffiest eyelids I'd ever seen. Later, I'd learn puffy eyelids are an indication of grief, feeling like sandy grit. The class was almost 50 people, a couple of teenagers 16+, otherwise included a wide array of people from healers and rapid eye technicians to those suffering from debilitating diseases and conditions. I essentially knew none of them.

We had just been divided into two groups, men downstairs and women upstairs. We began talking when Lynell suddenly looked at me and said, "I don't know what's going on right now, Elisa, but your sister is standing next to me, tapping on my head, and saying now is the time. You have to let her go."

My head snapped towards her, "Wait what? What do you mean, let her go?"

"Your grief was so much. You've been energetically holding your sister here. It's time for her to go; she has 6 hours. You must let her go," she says. "You need to cry and let it out."

I looked around the room, all eyes on me, and suddenly started sobbing again, huge, racking sobs. My body shook, my voice shook, I couldn't hold it in anymore. Suddenly, I was wailing and being led to the center of the room. Lynell began instructing people to send me energy, showing them the Cho Ku Rei reiki symbol and having them send it to me over and over.

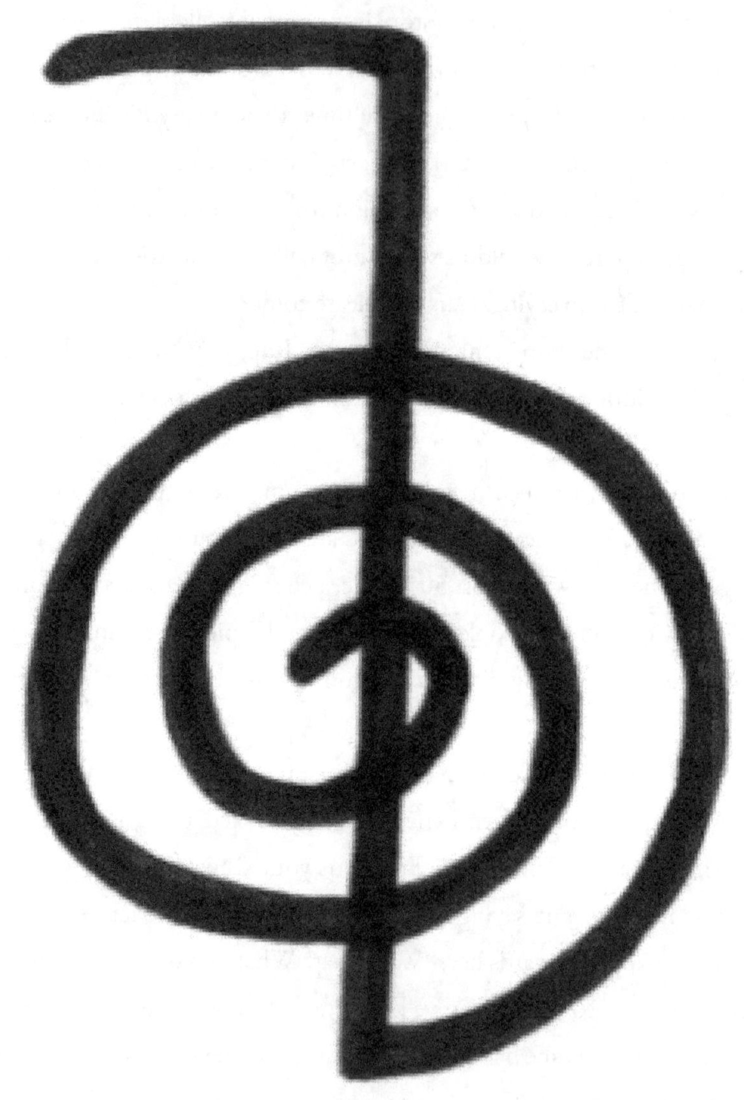

CHO KU REI

Cho Ku Rei is an ancient Chinese power symbol which means 'Placing all the power of the Universe here and now.' It indicates power and action and represents strong energy and action with direction and purpose.My Mom and Michidawn began raising my LOC (Level of Consciousness) assisting in the process of releasing the grief while supporting me.

After what felt like an eternity, the heavy and extreme sadness was suddenly gone. Windy...was gone. And with her, a painful heartache I'd been holding onto.

An hour later, my puffy eyelids were back to normal.

"I know what's causing some of your pain." I heard as I turned around to see who'd been speaking to me. "When you were going through that process earlier, your sister showed me what's going on with the pain in your chest. I can help if you'd like."

Her name was Tracy Gibbons, and I'd later learn she was another incredibly gifted intuitive and healer specializing in past lives and psychic clearings. What she saw during my earlier process was my past life in Egypt. One in which she said I was so powerful, they had me killed.

She said I was buried alive in that lifetime with scarabs, nasty beetles that eat and burrow into your flesh. A description I had just used the night before to describe the pain as if something was burrowing into me. Beyond the grave, they placed a scarab curse attached to my energetic soul, following me into multiple other lifetimes.

"Oh my God, that would be amazing," I said. "Let's meet." I gathered my Mom and Michidawn in our meeting room.

Sitting on a chair facing Tracy, she placed her hands on my heart and back.

"What happened in 2016?" she asked. "I'm seeing a tear in your energy field, a shattering. It allowed this curse to activate."

"Umm, the only thing I can think of is when I had my lower back/gluteal injury, I said. I had foot drop and could barely stand for more than 30 seconds at a time for over a week. It was a really bad injury. I couldn't even work out for at least two months following. About one or two weeks before it happened,

I'd consciously decided to stay at my job and not pursue becoming a writer or speaker."

"That incident is what allowed this curse to come in. The good thing is I know how to remove it," she said, smiling.

With Mom and Michidawn assisting Tracy energetically, I underwent another removal process. This time the removal of the scarab curse.

Asking Archangel Michael and Jofiel to assist in the process, Tracy kept her hands over the affected area on my chest and back, intending and using her 3rd eye to visually watch it release, all while Mom and Michidawn kept my Level of Consciousness (LOC) as high as possible. I remember feeling the curse lift and rise out, and suddenly I began sobbing. The pain completely changed for the better. It was still there, but not in the way I'd been experiencing, and certainly not in the same horrific way as before. I no longer had to lay on my right side and let the arm flop forward or backward. I could finally lay on both sides and do things I hadn't been able to do for almost a year.

Another miracle...

The next day the group was outside for a group activity we had just finished and were discussing. At one point, something was said to which I replied, "I've been calling in a team of people who want to work with me, using and feeling the gratitude I have for them."

"Elisa, I'm not sure you understand the depths or reach of your future work," Lynell replied, "It's far greater than anything you can fathom and will impact the world over," she said.

I didn't know how to respond. Instead, I simply nodded.

Later in the week, I had a name reading done, a process where the practitioner reads the energy meaning of each name, different for every name and person. In it, she said my soul was here to do the impossible and that I needed to reframe it to "I'm possible."

She also told me success would come when I was completely healed.

Later, I had someone come up and ask about my business, as she kept seeing a man who was both a future investor and business partner of mine.

I completely forgot about this until months later.

Towards the end of the week, I was enjoying my 4:00 AM shower when I suddenly felt an energetic punch to the gut, almost taking me to my knees. This was followed by the immediate thought to share my most recent experience; of meditation, my mood, and the impact it's had on my blood pressure, lab work, and overall health; with those at the retreat.

And, I'd recently been told by the Tibetan Bowl practitioner, that when I get a gut punch, I'd better listen.

Feeling incredibly nervous, I approached Lynell prior to class starting.

"Hey Lynell, I'm hoping to share something with the class if that's OK with you," I said.

"Of course," she replied. "We'll have you speak before the Skills Lecture".

The Skills for Life classes were developed by Ranae, the Rapid Eye technology founder, and are a series of lectures about the tools and life skills we have available to each and every one of us. They are the Universal laws and principles we all live by."

My nerves were through the roof when my time came, but I stood in front of the room.

"I'm not sure why I'm supposed to be telling you this, but I was very firmly told this morning in my shower that I need to tell my story.

"The last few months have been a huge transformational time for me. I quit my job in January and essentially left traditional medicine. Following my intuition that I needed to go within, I've been learning how to meditate and access other dimensions and levels."

"The last few months have completely changed me. I'm a different person. I'm more patient and calmer (even my family has noticed and remarks on it), and I do everything possible to be in coherence, trusting my inner voice and knowing."

"And I know I'm a Master of Inner Health," I said, feeling the power in the statement as I said it. "Though I'm at the tip of the iceberg in mastering it in this lifetime."

I glanced at Lynell, who was nodding her head in agreement.

"And that's it," I said. I just felt compelled to let you all know.
With that, I sat down.

Chapter Five

*D**ark Night of the Soul.*

When it rains, it pours.

One week after returning from Souls, I was scheduled to have surgery on my knee. Upon returning, I remember thinking I didn't feel as elevated, free, clear, or happy as I'd been before, leading up to, and while at Souls. I didn't feel as good or connected as I'd been for over three months. Something had changed.

I was also in the middle of constructing my website and marketing for my new business *Bodhi*. While at Souls, I'd agreed to pay $26,000 to a new marketing company, believing I'd soon have patients, clients, and money rolling in, which we desperately needed. By my calculations, our reserves were set to run out by mid-July or the beginning of August. And I was jumping all in.

On July 6th, I had surgery to repair the lateral meniscus of my left knee.

One week later, I was filming the first four episodes of my Quantal U series.

Life was picking up steam, and I couldn't be more excited. This was it. It was finally happening.

Little did I know, our family was entering the start of the most difficult period in our lives.

On July 15th, my website went live, and on August 1st, Quantal U, Episode One premiered entitled; *The Missing Link in Traditional Medicine.*

The response was underwhelming, to say the least, and definitely not what we needed to pay our monthly bills. To add insult to injury, Freedom CBD was quickly going downhill, and Brian was bringing in no money from them either. We'd be in big trouble if we didn't figure out something quick.

Unfortunately, this being Brian's umpteenth company going under and him dealing with very toxic behaviors from those he worked with, Brian wasn't faring well. Most mornings he spent meditating for two to three hours at a time, just to get in a space to get out of bed and do whatever possible to *do* something. The truth was, he was overwhelmed with the shame, guilt, pain, and loss of another company. And his confidence was non-existent due to working alongside a psychotic narcissist for too many years. Someone who used words, manipulation, and verbal and emotional abuse to control and demean every person or employee he worked with. Brian included.

And it had taken its toll. Our family wasn't dealing with one major life crisis. We were dealing with several. My career change, financial income drop, and mid-life crisis. Brian's loss of another company, lack of financial income, and his own mid-life crisis.

Most importantly, the direct impact of having an oppositional defiant child in our family affecting our daily lives.

It was the darkest of times.

Taylor, my oldest was now 15, soon to be 16. From the day she was born, she's been a spitfire, determined, incredibly smart, empathic, and full of high energy. She wanted to check out *everything*, and I mean everything, all at once. At around 8-9 months, when she started crawling, she stopped cuddling or putting her head on our shoulders as she was always, constantly in motion, and never wanted to miss a thing, insisting she be facing out at all times. If she was awake, she was investigating, not cuddling. The only time she'd let me was when I'd hold her while she had her bottle before a nap or bedtime, though she still didn't lay her head on our shoulders.

This finally changed around 18 months. Taylor was with Brian in Idaho for a week while he was working, and I was back in Kirksville in the middle of my first year of medical school. Unfortunately, Taylor had been dealing with rotavirus for several days. That week alone, I had a biochemistry test, an Anatomy and physiology test, an Osteopathic Manipulative Medicine (OMM) test, and an OMM practical. It was a busy week.

Though she was still playing and acting OK, Taylor had several bouts of diarrhea and had lost noticeable weight. She and Brian were to fly home, but he didn't feel he could get her on the plane as she was having too many diarrhea and vomiting spells. I was starting to worry she was becoming dehydrated, and I needed to be with my child. On Sunday, I contacted Ron Gaber, our Dean of students (and one of my greatest advocates) and let him know I needed to go be with her. Then I booked a flight and drove three hours to the Kansas City airport to catch a flight to Boise. When I arrived that night around 10 pm, Taylor was already asleep. I quietly entered the bedroom where she was staying and sleeping. Reaching into the crib, I picked her up. She initially squirmed, looked up at me, and, as soon as she realized who it was, dropped her head on my shoulder, holding me tight. She hadn't done that in months. I could feel the weight she'd lost, her tiny body fragile and thin. There she rested for over an hour before I finally put her back down.

Since that time, she started cuddling and laying her head on us again. It was a beautiful moment.

Being the oldest cousin on both sides of her family, Taylor was a natural leader, organizer, and creator of all things fun. She usually had to be in charge, often causing drama with her cousins and sisters. All in all though, her ideas were met with resounding excitement. With her cousins, she created a group called the "Funsies" and made numerous Musically's, TikTok's, and other fun videos, all in the name of a good time.   She was never short of ideas.

Taylor also loved to dance. She started ballet at age 3 and quit at 5 as it was too boring. This led her to take tumbling classes, where she had natural ability, and leading her to receive an invitation to join a competitive tumbling team at the age of 8. This introduction to competitive dance was all she needed; from then on, it became all she wanted to do, including ballet. She loved it and, all in all...was happy.

Unfortunately, or fortunately, as it wouldn't have brought us to where we are today, everything changed in May of 2017 when my sister Windy passed away.

Windy was two years my younger sister. My birthday is 11/17/78, while hers was 11/4/80. She was the fourth child and second daughter.

Until the age of 9, we lived in McCall, ID, where the forest was truly our playground. Windy and I played with frogs, ants, snakes, and other creatures on a daily basis and used the woods behind our house to let our imaginations roam. I was very matter-of-fact. The typical, bossy older sister who liked to tell her, and everyone else, what to do, and how to do it. She was younger and kinder, softer in her approach, and shyer. More introverted. She had a gentleness about her that others felt, yearned for, and enjoyed whenever around her; they never doubted her intention. Her laugh was infectious, engaging, and beautiful.

As all big sisters do, I'd relentlessly torture them (more fun than mean), often putting them in a dark closet until they did or said what I wanted or tickle them until they couldn't take it anymore. We were close, though we had typical sibling fights and warfare.

Windy was also my protector at night between the ages of 7 to 9. If I was getting up to use the restroom, she'd have to go with me. Multiple times, in the middle of the night, I remember standing in the opening of our shared bedroom, the bathroom, a diagonal jump from our room. Windy would already be standing there calmly.

"Jump, Elisa, it's fine. I'm right here," she'd whisper.

At the same time, I'd be doing a "one, two, three" in my head as my body would sway and move in that direction with each subsequent number, as if I needed the extra inertia to get me there.

She'd sometimes wait several minutes, always patient, for me to be brave enough to finally jump. My younger, more graceful, more etheric sister, and my protector against the unseen.

As we grew older, we remained in each other's lives. She even coming from Ontario, OR, to visit me in Kirksville, MO, when I attended Truman State University. And I visited her when she attended school at Bringham Young University, ID. She also lived her summer semester between freshman and sophomore year with my brother Ken and me in our rental house on 19th St, in Boise, ID. It was the summer of 2000 and was, for all intents and purposes, a transformational and life-changing summer for us all.

Summer 2000 was the beginning of my relationship with my husband, Brian, and Windy's relationship with her husband, Nick. Needing money for school, Ken and I encouraged Windy to come and live with us and get a job at DIRECTV for the summer as a DIRECTV customer service representative. Her future husband, Nick, was in her training class.

I'd been working at DIRECTV since February 1999. Before that, I had just moved to Boise from Kirksville, where I'd attended Truman State University for a year and a half.

Little did I know what the Universe had in store.

Four weeks later, I was sitting in a training room at DIRECTV, and approximately nine months after that, I was placed on a team with my new boss, Brian Peavey.

In May of 2000, a few weeks before Windy would arrive, I remember telling my good friend I had a crush on him.

She was surprised. "He's not at all your type," she said, pointing to the fact I typically date athletes known for their looks and muscular physiques.

And she was right, of course. Brian, at that time in his life, and by my standards, did not meet the physical requirements I typically looked for in someone I dated. He was only 29 but had already lived a lifetime, having gotten sober from alcohol addiction in 1994.

While his sobriety was a true blessing, it brought with it a long road of recovery and healing. Brian had been drinking fairly regularly since he was 14 while living in Indonesia with his younger sister Jennifer and a host family. His Dad, Art, lived five hours away in a remote jungle location where he worked as a civil engineer for Morrison Knudsen (MK). Brian's Mom, Judy, was back in the States, nursing her wounds after their painful and bitter divorce.

The drinking started at 14 and worsened as he got older. By the time he got to college, his recollections included multiple nights of blacking out or waking in random places. His buddies always remarked that "Peavey always knew how to have a good time."

Brian's sobriety came in 1994 following a DUI, his Mom's push for the family to have an intervention and a 30-day stint in a rehab facility.

When he came out of rehab, Brian was a changed man, and he knew he was an alcoholic. It was not a life he wanted to go back to.

Unfortunately, the alcohol use was covering an even more serious issue, the fact that Brian was depressed, and not just any depression. He was diagnosed with bipolar depression. Brian stayed in bed for over a year following his recovery and hardly went out. This would go on for weeks at a time when suddenly he'd have a burst of activity, and for two to three days, he'd get many things done, barely sleeping during that time. His days of depression far outweighed the days of activity. Over time, he suffered from muscle atrophy, anxiety, overwhelm, fear, and dread.

Looking for a way to help, his Mom found Brian a dog, a golden retriever named Carlos. Like most animals, Carlos became his primary companion, taking on and helping disperse Brian's fears and emotions, often acting them out as skittish, nervous, and apprehensive about anything new. Eventually, Brian's psychiatrist found the right combination of medications that treated bipolar disorder, and Brian started to feel better.

Unfortunately, the side effects of the medications that helped him feel better included weight gain and moon facies. Over the next few years, Brian gained close to 75 lbs.

By the time he came to work at DIRECTV, it'd been almost four years since his sobriety. He'd applied for and gotten the job as a customer service representative and quickly rose through the ranks. He was good at what he did, smart, and college-educated. By the time I came to work with him, he'd been promoted to a Team Lead position. He was in charge of a Team of 13 customer retention representatives, of which I was a part.

I thought he was funny and nice, but stern. We laughed a lot together, got along well, and had an easy, casual rapport. A couple of months after being on the same team, Brian asked that I help him lose weight. He knew nutrition and health were a passion of mine, and he wanted to start feeling better again. We started talking more and more with regular conversations about health, exercise, what he should be eating, and what he needed to stop doing.

Brian stopped drinking Mountain Dew daily, began eating a healthier diet, and slowly started losing weight. After a while, we'd walk to lunch together to scope out what was healthy to eat. Our friendship blossomed, and I soon realized I had a new crush.

At the same time, my sister Windy was twitterpated herself.

On July 7th of 2000, Brian invited his DIRECTV team, and several friends, to a pool hall called Blue's Bouquet to celebrate his 30th Birthday. I was crushing hard, and I assume so was Brian. His good friend, Leila, also felt the connection.

When the bars closed, I invited Brian over for breakfast my cousin Tammy was making. He ended up staying until 6 am. We talked all night.

For the next several weeks, we talked over the phone for hours at a time. I remember seeing a nest of baby spiders had opened near the light on my ceiling. I watched them for four hours, crawling all over as I talked to Brian on the phone.

Eventually, we knew there was something more, and at the end of July, he kissed me for the first time. A week later, I quit DIRECTV as it was too difficult to be on his team, pretending there was no chemistry between us. It was so thick, it was palpable, as several people from our team would later tell us when we told them we were together.

On Christmas Day in 2000, Brian asked me to marry him, and I said yes. He'd already visited with my parents, asking their permission, and they gave their blessing. They'd have three children marrying that summer. My older brother Rob in May, myself on July 7, 2001, and my sister Windy on August 14th, 2001.

Over the next few years, I worked to complete my undergrad, and in May 2004, I graduated. Taylor Ann Peavey was born several months later on September 28th, weighing 7lbs 10 oz. Her delivery was uneventful, empowering, perfect, and amazing. I absolutely loved every aspect of being a Mom.

Less than four weeks later, I was interviewing to attend medical school in Kirksville at ATSU-KCOM. I received my acceptance a few days later.

To say med school was difficult is an understatement. I easily studied 80 hours/week and still only graduated in the middle of my class. This was a criterion that I continued to judge myself against, as my Dad had been in the top 10% of his medical school class.

During my second year of school, I became pregnant again, and in May of 2007, I failed my step one boards. I'd have to retake them after our new arrival was born.

On August 1, 2007, at the end of my second year of medical school, Isabella Grace (Bella) was born, weighing in at 7 lbs. 9 oz. As with Taylor, my labor was fairly uneventful, and the delivery one of the most empowering experiences of my life. It is one of the reasons I decided to go into OB, to begin with. If I could give women a small glimpse of the confidence that comes from an empowering labor, I wanted to do everything possible to make it happen.

Minutes after she was born, I remember looking at her and thinking, "my grace, I could do this all over again."

Nine days later, we flew cross country to Idaho, as we were temporarily homeless. The last year, to make things exciting, we decided to build a house, figuring it would make money when we sold it. We had rented the house we were currently living to an incoming medical school family and we had to be out before our new house was finished.

Storing all our stuff in the new garage, we flew to Idaho for a week to see family. I was determined to clear any and all influences that may have been impacting my ability to effectively take my boards. Searching around, my Mom found a Rapid Eye technician in McCall, ID, where I could do several sessions.

When we returned to Missouri, the house wasn't complete. We ended up staying at one of our WorldMark Resorts in Branson, MO, for a week, followed by another week of living in a hotel back in Kirksville. At the time, I was taking care of a newborn, breastfeeding, and studying for the boards I was taking again in September, all of which were happening in a single hotel room with three other people.

Our lives were busy! Thankfully, two weeks later, I successfully passed my Step 1 Boards.

Emiline Eileen Peavey (Emi) was born almost two years later, on July 20, 2009. We didn't know we wanted another. In fact, we were fairly certain we wouldn't be having another. But Emi had other plans, and to say she was a part of her creation is a definite understatement.

I didn't use birth control, as I didn't like the side effects, but we were very careful not to get pregnant. During the entirety of our marriage, unless pregnant or trying to become pregnant, we never had intercourse without a condom.

But the night Emi came to be, was easily in our top five moments of intimacy and connection. The intense and passionate emotion that overtook us took all thoughts of protection completely out of our minds.

And two weeks later, I was pregnant. The news of which came soon after the financial crash of 2008, the emotional and financial weight the heaviest I'd ever experienced up to that point in our lives.

How would we survive? Thankfully I had two months of extra maternity, saved from when I had Bella, and took a year off.

We somehow survived, despite the massive financial loss we'd just suffered. It wasn't easy but thankfully between the job Brian picked up at ATSU, my financial aid, and help from family, we managed. Though it was the lowest of lows.

In May of 2010, I graduated from medical school, the year being one of the most stressful. I again struggled with passing my Step Two boards, having to take them three times before finally passing, my belief in myself and my abilities shattered.

On top of that, our credit was tanked, we had hardly any money, and I couldn't complete on-site rotations (how we earn our spots as future residents) with a newborn requiring sustenance only I could give her. Not matching into OB as I wanted, I had to scramble and found a position in the OSU-Tulsa Family Medicine Residency.

In hindsight, it was a blessing I didn't match into OB, God knowing family medicine was a better fit. I loved procedures and deliveries, but I wasn't a surgeon. Most importantly, I lived and breathed preventative medicine, which I'd be better at doing in family medicine versus obstetrics. And, of course, I could always deliver as a family doc.

It was going to be okay, but 2010 was a difficult year.

By 2012, I was going into my final year of residency. Windy had finished her undergraduate degree and had gotten an additional degree in radiology/CT, working a full-time job, in the radiology department, at the local hospital. She also had two incredible little boys, the youngest only a year old in July of 2012. Dealing with PCOS (Polycystic Ovarian Syndrome) it took Windy and her husband several years to finally conceive, happening only after she began taking a natural progesterone cream to help balance her hormones. Until then, she was barely having a period every few months.

In December 2012, my extended family and I planned a vacation for us to meet at Disney World for a week. While there, Windy discovered abnormal bloody discharge from her nipple, and she was still breastfeeding her youngest. When arriving home, she scheduled an appointment with her doctor, and we knew her diagnosis by February. Stage IV, triple-negative breast cancer, the most aggressive type, with 32 positive lymph nodes in her left armpit and a CT scan that lit up her chest. Her oncologist told her she was palliative and gave her 3–5 years survival, with chemotherapy, if she was lucky.

But Windy didn't want 3-5 years. She wanted to live for as long as possible. She wanted to beat cancer, which she knew *was* possible, through diet and other integrative healing methods.

Thus began Windy's cancer battle. She started looking into various therapies and saw that the Gerson therapy had several successful stories of cancer remission, doing this protocol. It consisted of several, sometimes 10+ juices throughout the day and 10+ coffee enemas each day. Several per day.

To learn the protocol and become efficient at it, Windy visited the Gerson Center in Mexico, where she stayed with my Mom for three weeks. There she met many others in various stages and types of cancer development. One particular gal was from Australia and had been diagnosed with melanoma, a survival rate not often exceeding five years. They became fast friends and she still keeps in touch with my mom today.

Over the next 2 years, the diet and enemas took most of her time and planning, especially as the juices needed to be consumed within ten minutes to have the best effect, and each enema lasted 20-30 minutes. It was time-consuming and was a full-time job in and of itself.

To accommodate her time, Windy had to leave her job, and she and her husband moved to a house on my parent's farm with their boys.

Six months after starting treatments, Windy had an updated CT scan. Her scan previously showed a large mass in her armpit (32 positive lymph nodes discovered during her mastectomy), which had shrunk by 1-2 mm. It also showed several chest nodules that couldn't be seen on the new scan.

Put simply, Windy had no signs of metastasis, and the metastases that were seen in the prior scan were no longer visible. The diet and enemas were working.

I graduated from Residency in June 2013, and we moved to Ontario soon after. Over the next couple of years, Windy and I saw each other often, sometimes daily, even joining forces to start a home school we called Paideia. Our kids grew closer to each other and their aunts and uncles. This included Taylor with her Aunt Windy, and many times over the next few years, especially after we'd moved to Bend, she would spend a day or two, at a time, with Aunt Windy. She loved her more than anything, even holding a fund-raiser to help raise money for her very expensive treatments.

It was no surprise then that Taylor would be devastated by Windy's passing, even lending herself to a mic drop moment at the funeral. However, no one could have predicted where that would lead.

In May 2016, Windy finished her two years of Gerson therapy and was feeling great. We even went to dinner to celebrate this monumental moment. One month later, she noticed some lymph node enlargement along the side of her neck and started having a mild cough. Repeat scans indicated the cancer had returned, once again showing positive chest nodules and lymph node involvement.

On the search for other treatment options, Windy began working with a holistic physician in Reno, NV, who had tested her cancer against certain new therapies, finding therapeutic chemotherapy with a 90% cure rate. To get this therapy, she'd need to have a port in place, a device that allows easy access to her venous system for therapeutic and IV support. Unfortunately, it also increases one's risk for a serious infection in the blood.

On Wednesday, May 24th, 2017, I received a call from my Mom saying Windy was going to the hospital. She was hurting, weak, and didn't feel good. Once there, they determined she had sepsis, an infection of the blood. They were starting antibiotics, and we were waiting to see if they would help.

Taylor had just left with her 7th-grade class for a two-day overnight adventure called Greek Olympiad. She'd be back on Friday. On Thursday morning, I left my house for work when Mom called again, "The doctor says she's not going to make it," she said. "He says the infection has caused her liver, kidneys, and body to shut down. She doesn't have much longer. You should come."

I immediately turned around, drove home, and packed a quick meager stash of clothes and toiletries, then jumped in my car for the 5-hour trip to Boise. I had to make it in time. Around the time I reached Millican, I realized I didn't have much gas left, and I stopped to get some. I walked into the store/restaurant, bursting with the smells of breakfast. "I'm hoping to get some gas," I said to the guy behind the counter.

"We don't sell gas here. The closest place to get it is Burns unless the guy in Brother's is selling gas today. Never know." He shrugged.

I'd have to make a decision.

By calculation, I'd be over 20 miles shy of what I needed to make it to Burns, where I *knew* there was gas. But I was already 45 miles in and wasn't turning around. I needed to get to Boise and see Windy before she passed. I prayed the guy in Brother's would be available.

"Thanks," I called as I walked out.

"Please, God, find me some gas," I muttered to myself under my breath.

I drove the next 15 minutes wondering if I'd made a huge mistake, I was taking a risk, and it was a big one. Drive back to Bend and lose several additional hours or drive on and pray the Universe was there to assist.

As I pulled into Brothers, I saw no one. The front door was locked tight with a closed sign on the door. What was I going to do?

I drove to the gas area, parked, put my head back, and closed my eyes. "Please, God," I said. "Help me get there in time."

I opened my eyes and looked. Suddenly behind the buildings, I saw a man riding on his 4-wheeler. He was headed my way.

He was older, mid-sixties most likely, and balding.

"Hey there!" I said, "I'm hoping to get some gas."

He eyed me up and down and replied, "I'm not typically open this time. You're lucky to see me", he said. "Do you have cash? I prefer cash."

"I don't have cash," I replied. "Is there any way you can take a credit card? Or can I send you money? Please, I need to get to Boise as soon as possible."

"The card machine charges a hefty interest, and I have to go get it. Gas is $5/gallon," he said, quoting a price almost double our current gas prices. He was a true Godsend in every sense of the word. I could make it to Boise without running out of gas.

Several hours later, I arrived at the hospital and found most of my brothers and sisters already there. Windy's eyes fluttered open groggily as I entered her ICU hospital room and she reached out to me. "I love you," she said simply, and she smiled.

I immediately hugged and laid my head on her chest. "I love you so much, Windy. It's OK to go. It's OK to be free. Free of your pain, free from this disease," I said, sobbing. I promise we'll do everything we can to take care of your boys. They'll always know how much their Mom loved them," I said.

Windy was in and out of consciousness, unable to converse.

We sat with her for another few hours, taking turns at her bedside, crying together in the gathering room.

Windy passed away peacefully at 6:55 pm on May 25th, 2017. At the moment of her passing, I was a spiritual witness to those gathered to welcome her home, including several family members who'd passed before her. My Grandpa Mairs, along with my Grandma Raison, Uncle Hugh, and many others as well. She was no longer in pain. She was now at peace.

But the grief was all-consuming. My younger sister was dead. I was a doctor, and I couldn't save her. When I called my husband, we decided to wait and tell Taylor the next day. We didn't want her to be alone, without family, when she heard the news. Brian would tell her when he picked her up from school the next day.

There have been *many* times since this moment that I've wished it never went this way, times I wish I could have done better, been better, known better how to grieve. Known better what my child would need when she found out her Aunt had passed away.

However, I know that without this experience, we'd not be where we are today. I would not have the family I do now.

But I can honestly say this is one of my life's hardest and most difficult experiences because it directly affected our entire family almost daily for several years. Like tar that slowly seeps into your lives, and before you know it, you're covered and can barely scrape it off. This is how the experience was for me. I don't wish it on anyone else. But I am also eternally grateful for where it's brought us.

When Brian told Taylor that Windy had passed away, Taylor said she'd never felt more anger at anyone in her entire life than she was at me, in that moment.

Anger with a low enough frequency to allow a psychic attack on my daughter.

A psychic attack meaning a low frequency entity/energy wishing only to harm.

One that was strong enough to affect her personality, her thoughts, her feelings about herself and others (including me), and over time, her self-confidence.

At first, we chalked up the change in behavior to her age. She was 13, going on 14, and was in the prime of her adolescence. And she had *always* been a strong-willed child. We were destined to have a strong-willed adolescent as well.

Right? It wouldn't be until years later, I'd finally come to learn the real reason for her anger.

After several months, I also began to notice changes in my daughter Bella. She felt less confident in herself, which was noticeable in her school, dance, and friends. One of her best friends quickly became friends with Taylor and stopped being friends with her. I noticed that Taylor seemed to revel in hurting Bella's feelings or making her feel "less than." It didn't matter how much I'd speak to Taylor to quit and/or try to smooth things over, I slowly watched my Bella Boo begin to sink into herself. Having seen and taken care of many depressed teenagers, I vowed to do any and everything to get my kids the most effective help. I started having her work with a lady who used to be a Rockette but who has now found her spiritual purpose, creating programs and working directly with young dancers.

Gina and Bella worked well together, and as the months passed, she began gaining her confidence again. It was about this time Taylor stopped messing with her as much. She was moving on to easier targets...Me.

The tension between Taylor and me began to escalate in 2018. She became more disrespectful when fighting, hardly took responsibility, picked incessantly on her sisters, always had to be in control, and, more importantly, stopped apologizing, which was rare, to begin with.

The pattern of holding every outing or fun event over her head was a constant in our lives. She was continually being threatened she couldn't go somewhere and/or punished for having done something, said something unkind, or lied about something that happened.

And wow, did she lie. I'd venture to guess she was lying around 80% of the time, if not more. It seemed second nature.

Not only did she lie, but she knew how to manipulate and work the system. She knew all the buttons to push, who to go to for what, and what to say to each parent to get what she wanted.

By late summer of 2018, I was beginning to wonder when she'd turn the "adolescent corner" as our fights had gotten worse. She didn't want to hear any of my opinions, never wanted me around, and, most of all, didn't believe in God, Spirit, Magic, or the Universe.

"I stopped believing in all of it as soon as Windy died!" she screamed one evening when I was discussing the impact of her negative thoughts on her life.

"If it was real, "she'd still be alive!" Taylor screamed, stomping out of the room.

I stood there and didn't follow. Because what do you say to that? How do you tell a child their Aunt left because it was her time to leave, that she, her OverSoul and the Individual Soul Ray life 'Windy'; chose this exit point for her life?

How was I able to tell her such a thing when I didn't even know if I believed it myself. I was beyond sad she'd left behind her two little boys and I felt we had failed the emotional and energetic healing approach; which prior to her death, I felt certain could heal any dis-ease process, cancer included. Especially when done at the right time, with the right circumstances, and of course...with an absolute belief or faith in it happening.

For me, it was another failure and I had nothing to show to prove the contrary. Her Aunt Windy was dead, and we didn't save her.

In 2019, in desperation she'd see the light, I made Taylor attend Souls with Stamina, with my Mom, for the week. She was so mad at me for sending her, she refused to speak or communicate with me for over two weeks. When I saw her in Florida for a month of intensive summer dancing, she continued to talk back, manipulate, and speak negatively about Bella and me to her friends, who were there with us.

The wall between us felt bigger than ever, and I was starting to feel I'd never get back to a "relationship" with my daughter. It was devastating.

Over the next year, the relationship and her behavior worsened. She'd test our limits and boundaries, and a massive fight would ensue if told no. No fight ever came to a resolution; subsequently, we'd go days not speaking. During that time, Brian (as a defense mechanism and because it's how he avoids conflict) would act with her as if there had been no fight or tension. I'd be the only one unable to act as if nothing had happened.

It created a lot of isolation and family division. I'd typically exit the room when Taylor was around as the tension was beyond palpable. Bella, Emi, and Brian were exhausted from hearing and feeling it as well. When Taylor was at work, it would be the four of us. There are few pictures of the five of us during that time, as we were often not all together or happy when we were together.

In September 2020, two weeks before Taylor's 16th birthday, my friend Hector was in town to film several more interviews for my Quantal U series.

I can't remember why but Taylor had just lost her phone, iPad, and internet privileges for disobeying her father and me. She would only be allowed to have them for whatever schoolwork she was doing. At the time, she had around two hours of work to do, for which we agreed to give her the phone from 9-11 pm. But this wasn't good enough for her, and she fell back on one of her typical strategic attacks.

Keep asking, and don't relent.

"Mom, why can't I have it? This isn't fair. Everyone else gets their stuff! This is child abuse. I'm going to call the cops. Give back my fucking stuff!!!, she screamed!"

"Mom! Mom! Mom! Mom!" she said over and over.

I continued to ignore her when suddenly, I felt the moment it happened. She snapped.

"What the FUCK!!!" she screamed. This is all your fault. You're the reason this is happening. I hate you! You're the reason I hate myself, hate you, and hate my life!!!! You're the worst mom ever!!! Everything is your fault. You suck!"

She continued with a similar rant for another 30 minutes, screaming as loudly as possible.

Everything was in slow motion, and I felt like I was seeing everything as it happened in her head, when and why she suddenly snapped, her directed and manipulated assaults...*everything!*

I was shocked. It had never been this bad before. She was full-on attacking me at the deepest and lowest level she possibly could.

No amount of conversation, begging, trying to explain, or communicating helped.

We went to bed, unresolved, and the next morning I left for two days with Hector for interviews.

Chapter Six

Shortly after Hector left for home, Brian and I decided to move from Bend. We didn't have the income to continue paying our rent or all our bills, and due to COVID, our girls were doing school from home.

We figured this would be the perfect opportunity to "have an adventure," save money, and do something we wouldn't otherwise.

The next two months consisted of the arduous process of selling as much as we could that we didn't need. We sold multiple pieces of furniture, including our couch, cabinets, plant stands, cedar chests, buffet tables, dressers, bunk beds, you name it. We got rid of clothes we didn't need, décor we didn't use, and multiple other items we dragged around with us from place to place.

I even sold my car, my baby. A Lincoln MKZ with all the perks, bells, and whistles that I had just paid off.

Using the money I got from it, we purchased a 2012 Honda Odyssey. Funnily, I'd always vowed to *never* own a mini-van. LOL!

Ultimately, we were getting rid of the old and making way for the new.

Sometime around October I began having worsening left sided neck, chest, and scapular pain that often radiated down into my left shoulder and arm. The muscle tightness and somatic dysfunction was often bad enough I remember having the distinct thought that it felt as if I was hanging from a wall via a large hook that was pierced through my body.

Knowing Tracy Gibbons' psychic gift for past lives and feeling somehow like this was connected I reached out to her asking if she would swap sessions with me and she immediately agreed.

The next day we connected via phone while she tapped in to what she could see.

Tracy

So I'd like to walk you through the process and see what comes up as I've gotten several hits and want to see what information you can add, OK? I'll talk through what I am seeing and will ask you questions. Say the first thing that comes to mind and don't over think it OK? I've been feeling/seeing a past life around the 1400 -1500's and I'm seeing you on a horse with an army of soldiers.

Are you male of female?

Elisa

Female.

Tracy

OK. You're headed somewhere specific. Are you the leader?

Elisa

Umm, yes think I am. I feel as if I'm in charge. I can see me on a horse and feel others behind me.

Tracy

OK yes that was what I was getting too. So what I'm seeing/feeling is that in this lifetime you suffered some horrendous injury or torture.

Elisa

Wow, yes it feels like that. Like a large hook has pierced through my left chest and I'm hanging from it, my body feels completely mangled and almost broken. It's the weirdest feeling. I feel like I'm being torn apart.

Tracy

It's because you're processing one of your past lives, where you were brutally tortured. In that lifetime you were a warrior and led an army of people. Unfortunately, you were captured and tortured.

Tracy's words were ringing true and I began having thoughts to the fact she was talking about Joan of Arc, now the second time I've had thoughts and/or a feeling of a connection with this incredible woman.

Tracy

How about we let that go now? As there is no reason to hang on to such a traumatic experience. How do you feel about thanking God for the lesson and allowing the trauma to pass?

Elisa

(very enthusiastically)

Yes, please!!

Tracy

We're watching, observing, and feeling the release. Thanking your soul for the lesson and allowing the pain, trauma, and imprint of the experience to let go. Allowing your musculoskeletal system to find its way back to perfection and wholeness.

(I take a deep breath in and slowly blow out)

Tracy

How does that feel?

Elisa(says astonishingly)

Much better! I can already start to feel the muscles begin to relax and let go.

Tracy

Perfect! I want you to go easy the next few days, don't overdo it. We've cleared a lot of stuff today and it will take several days to allow it all to settle. Let's check in next week and see how you're feeling.

Elisa

Sounds great!

Over the next few days the pain and somatic dysfunction continued to improve and I began to feel a little better.

In November 2020, two days before my 42nd birthday, we officially left Bend for good, something Taylor was *not* happy about. From her perspective, we were once again interrupting and changing her world and moving.

Planning to stay in Bend until the girls graduated high school, we had told her this wouldn't happen until she'd already left home.

But we didn't plan on Covid happening and changing everything.

Unfortunately, for Taylor, it didn't matter. She was angry, and she honestly had valid points.

We'd had several major moves in her life. The first, when we moved from Kirksville, MO, to Tulsa, OK, she sobbed and cried as we left town.

When we planned to move from Tulsa to Ontario in 2013 when I finished residency, she didn't want to leave her dance family and favorite teachers. For weeks, she talked about not moving and staying instead. The only saving grace was promising we'd finally be home with family.

But when Ontario didn't work out after two years, we picked up once again and moved to Bend.

Bend was the fourth new dance studio and the fifth new school, and Taylor had a hard time adjusting. It took her almost six months to put herself out there in dance and get to know the team.

So, when we decided to move again, she was angry, adding tenfold to the tension already between us. It created multiple fights, concerns for an altercation when tempers became too high, and even a 911 call by Taylor herself after we refused to return her phone.

She quickly regretted the choice as she wanted to hang up almost as soon as the 911 operator answered the other line. Unfortunately, it was too late.

As it meant they'd send someone out to ensure everything and everyone was OK.

When the police came to the door Brian and I refused to speak with them, instead making her step outside and telling them why she called…she was mad we wouldn't give her phone and privileges back. Though an incident I prefer not to repeat, I was proud of her for taking responsibility when she went to speak with them, admitting that she was overreacting and being more than a bit melodramatic.

Soon however, Taylor began to threaten physical or verbal abuse over the smallest of incidents (such as when I reached for a bag she had with something I was confiscating and in the process of taking it she felt physically threatened) and we all began recording our fights. I soon worried whether she would make things up to get me in trouble. No car ride was peaceful. Nine times out of ten, we'd fight the entire time. There was no resolution and no end.

When we moved in November, we settled at my parent's house in Ontario through Christmas, planning to leave for our getaway destination in January. Brian and I wondered if Taylor should come with us as we worried we'd take her and it would be miserable for the entire family. If we had $40,000, we'd have sent her to a wilderness camp for troubled teens, but we only had access to a family counselor. She was wonderful; however, the conversations still didn't go anywhere. We wanted Taylor to be respectful, take responsibility for her actions, and be willing to apologize when she's done something wrong. Unfortunately, she was stubborn and unwilling to budge.

I felt hopeless, helpless, and unsure of what to do. If I'd been in any other relationship that felt this toxic, this belittling, and this difficult; I'd have dropped it years ago. But she was my child and my responsibility and even though she didn't like me, it was my job to ensure she was fed, clothed, and taken care of. At times I felt like a battered housewife, taking verbal beating after verbal beating and manipulation after manipulation; watching her poison her friends, sisters, and sometimes her dad with the language and words she spoke about me.

We didn't decide about Taylor until two days before we were to leave when she came and gave a half-hearted apology. But at least it was an apology, something she hadn't done in forever. She was coming with us.

When we first arrived at my parent's house, I was having a very difficult time spiritually. Between the end of March through the beginning of July 2020, I'd begun to grow my spiritual practice. I meditated almost daily, spoke regularly to my guides and began leaning into my feelings and intuition. I had also become adept at bringing in the emotion I preferred to feel, such as gratitude. As when we surround and *feel* our emotions, our body immediately begins to create circumstances that will bring more of that into our lives, creating more of that emotion and feeling.

It's universal law and one that Jesus speaks about in the bible. Two different versions of this statement exist, one from King James and one from the most recent Aramaic version, discovered in 1947.

The King James Version states, "Whatsoever ye ask the father in my name, he will give it to you. Ask, and ye shall receive and your joy may be full."

Comparatively, the Aramaic version says, "All things that you ask straightly, directly, from inside my name, you will be given. Ask without hidden motives and be surrounded by your answer. Be enveloped by what you desire, that your gladness be full."

Same passage, two completely different translations. The Aramaic version is telling us to "feel" the emotion we want to create, "feel" the desires we wish to manifest, and "feel" the emotion surrounding and enveloping us as this is how we manifest what we want to create.

Its Universal law.

Versus the King James Version where the instructions are simply to ask for what we want in Jesus's name.

The difference between the versions are a stark contrast to each other further confirming the intentional mistranslation of important, key and Universal truths.

In this case the Universal truth specific to how we truly manifest our desires, as we must *feel* them to create. When we feel our desires with emotion, the limbic system immediately sends those feelings via signals to the rest of the body putting out more energetic frequencies to create what we wish to bring into fruition.

And I had been doing that, but as soon as I returned from Souls that summer, I felt and knew that something had changed. I had a harder time connecting to those feelings. I felt less elevated, and by the time we showed up at my parent's house in November, I could barely feel any positive emotion.

And I certainly couldn't bring them out to feel them envelop me.

For all intents and purposes, I was in a dark void. However, I also felt pulled and compelled to learn more about who I was, my gifts, and what I came here to bring. Not only was I feeling this pull, I was receiving regular messages from online psychics in my email, all encouraging me to do the same. "Find out who you are," the subject lines would say. "You have gifts you don't know about. Call for a consultation."

Not knowing how to go about this and not having any money to spend for a consultation, I spent any free time I had, trying to meditate and connect again with myself. Most days I felt helpless and hopeless and began wondering if anything would ever change.

Dealing with regular left-sided neck pain, I'd often spend my time using the healing intention *ho'oponopono* to release the muscle tension. *Ho'oponopono* is a Hawaiian phrase that roughly translates "to move things back in balance or to make things right" and works by invoking the laws of forgiveness. Placing my hands over the area of muscle tightness and soreness, I say the words below with as much emotion and feeling as possible and repeat them over and over while moving my fingers to each sore area of muscles I can reach.

"I love you. Please forgive me. I'm so sorry. Please forgive all the insults. Please forgive all who've witnessed the insults, including God. Thank you."

As I say the words, I can feel the muscles squirm around, soften, and start to relax under my fingers. Sometimes the relief comes quickly, other times I have to say the affirmations over and over, it often being one of the only tools to bring relief.

But, towards the end of December 2020, I noticed something when saying these things. Each time I'd say, "Please forgive all those who've witnessed the insults, including God," I'd see in my mind's eye and felt compelled to add the name 'Jesus', starting me down the path of saying, "including God and Jesus."

Which was very odd. Though I greatly respected him, I also saw, knew and understood the illusion and manipulation most Christian and Catholic churches use in his name. But whenever I'd say God, Jesus would also pop into my head.

I also had thoughts around the idea that I was somehow a direct descendant or related to him somehow. I'm not sure how these came to me, but I thought of them. Then, just as quickly, I dismissed them.

In January of 2021, it was apparent my business was not moving forward, and I soon realized Quantal U would be coming to an end; I couldn't afford it anymore. My new vision was to create three, six, or nine-month life and health transformational programs for people. I'd been looking into different marketing methods and stumbled across a marketing ad for a company that looked incredibly promising. They had several well-known specialists and promised a return. All it would take was $10,000.

Feeling this would be the kick start I needed, my mom loaned me the money, and for the month of January, I worked to create the perfect online ads, funnels, discovery calls, and program for getting people to sign up for my programs. I worked every day, usually from 9 to 5, doing little to less of anything else. The work was tedious. Not only was this my first experience learning how to online market, create funnels, write ads, make web pages, and put them all together, but I was doing it all myself. I felt like I was in a vat of molasses, moving at turtle speed, only to have several hours' worth of work disappear or not take.

But I kept moving slowly. By the end of January, we were set to depart on our adventure. I had a couple weeks of work to do before promoting my new program. It seemed as if things were finally coming together.

Better yet, I was beginning to feel positive feelings again. The end of January marked a long end to several months of feeling almost nothing but dark and heaviness. It was finally starting to lift.

Packed into a black honda odyssey, our family of five headed out at the end of January. The first stop to see our good friends in Council Bluffs, IA, for a few days en route to Florida for the next several months.

We had a great visit and after decided to drive through and stay in Washington, DC. We'd never been and thought the kids would enjoy seeing the place where law and government came to be.

I was driving when we entered DC, but approximately 30 - 45 minutes from arrival, I noticed more tension in the car, less patience, more outbursts, and less communication and compromise. Aside from this, DC was nothing like we expected. It felt dark and dreary. Most of the capital and legislature buildings were encircled with wire fencing, keeping us out. The entryways were protected by the military and their guns.

Most people walking around were wearing not one but two masks, all avoiding eye contact and refusing to look at each other. The majority of restaurants were still closed from covid, and those that were open served smaller menus, mostly for pickup.

DC felt sick and dead.

By the time we got to the hotel and checked in Brian and I were in an all-out fight, and I honestly don't remember what about.

To this day, all I remember is it was the worst fight of our entire 20-plus years of marriage and being together. It was ugly; I said ugly things. Things I'd never dream of saying normally. At one point, I didn't think we could stay together, and worst of all, I didn't care much. I felt justified in my anger and simply wanted to fuck it all.

Finally, after no resolve, Brian left with the girls, staying with them in their room, and I hunkered down in ours. At some point, as I was lying there on the bed, I once again had a thought that'd come to me three or four other times that day, which was that we were under psychic attack. I also knew I had the power to get rid of them.

I closed my eyes and said, "I'm stepping into my circle of 100% pure healing light, Archangel Michael. I call on you to assist in removing any and all entities, energies, or influences from my field that aren't 100% for my highest and best. Take them where they'll no longer impact anyone else. It is Done. It is Done. It is Done!"

Suddenly I opened my eyes, and the room looked a bit brighter. Most importantly, the incessant, dark thoughts I'd been having over and over were gone. I felt like I had space in my brain again and felt immensely lighter. Wow, that was intense.

The next morning, Brian and I resolved the fight. Though the air was still heavy, it was much improved.

We were *all* ready to get the hell out of DC.

Instead of moving around multiple WorldMark resorts in different cities, we decided it would be easier to be in one place. That way, the girls could take dance classes, and Taylor could get a job, something we all knew would allow her a chance to earn money and give us a much-needed reprieve in our small apartment.

We settled on staying in Deerfield Beach, FL, approximately 45 minutes from Miami.

All in all, Florida was good for us. The girls continued with their online school, which started around noon every day, and Taylor got a job at a place called Papa's Raw Bar, working 20 to 30 hours per week. Brian was hired by a company called AIL at the end of January, selling life insurance policies, all commission based.

The job had a big learning curve, often taking years to truly develop a consistent, stable income.

While the future potential for an entrepreneur like Brian was promising, we had no idea how many years it would take to get there. The job, however, fulfilled his requirement of having his own business along with the support and leadership of a team.

In March of 2021, I had been unsuccessfully trying to have Facebook approve my ads to promote my program. I couldn't get any to go through for one reason or another. Soon my money ran out and I had no additional money to pay for ads and/or promote the program. One more failure to add to my growing list after thousands had been invested.

Feeling completely defeated, I didn't know what to do. I had been dealing with financial hardship and subsequent problems my entire life. I obviously had a pattern I needed to break, including feelings of lack. Feelings that obviously outnumbered any feelings I had around financial abundance and flow. But the truth is I had already done so much work surrounding abundance and vibing with the flow of money coming into my life. It seemed the number one thing I had been trying to work on and overcome was impossible to do.

In college, I worked three part-time jobs and could barely pay my bills. When I moved to Boise and worked at DIRECTV full-time, I made $10/hour or $1600 before taxes and around $1100 after. By the time my bills were paid, I was scraping the barrel. I remember having one pair of jeans that fit me until the night they busted open and were no more.

I realized I needed another job and began working at a pizza place in town. At $3.25/hour plus tips, it was often difficult to save anything, but I was at least paying all my bills. And I was single with no dependents.

Once Brian and I were married, we consistently had highs and lows of money in our account. Since Brian was a real estate investor, his income came from creating win-win real estate deals. When they came together, it wasn't uncommon to have $30,000, 40,000, or even $50,000 come into our account. Unfortunately, much of that would be an investment for other deals, paying contractors and subcontractors or paying other people their interest from investing. It seemed the high never lasted too long, and soon money was tight again until he could close the next one.

Financially, money was always in and out of our lives until the crash of 2008 when the ebbs and flows stopped altogether, leaving only the lows. It wouldn't be until years later that I'd truly understand the deeply rooted financial patterns and beliefs of lack I took on and developed as a child, which were still running my life rampant.

Completely defeated and with no further money to invest, I let go of the three, six, or nine-month program idea. I had *no* idea what God wanted me to do, and I felt it was entirely my fault. I had too much shame, too many doubts, and too many what if's, interfering with my ability to create the vision and life I wanted.

It was obvious my energy patterns of lack were too strong and held too much power to overturn. If I had just stayed positive, it would be much different. I was angry and upset at myself and didn't feel I could succeed. Instead, I wanted to end my life. I wasn't scared of dying; I knew what was on the other side. It was beautiful and freeing, instead of being held within a 3D construct, keeping us limited and unknowing.

At the time, we were on the 8th floor of WorldMark apartments in Deerfield Beach, and the thought came to me to jump off the side of the deck. It would be quick, fast, and should end me quickly.

Could I really do it? Could I really leave my kids? Leave my husband? They were the only ones keeping me here.

At the time, because of my relationship with Taylor, I often spent time away from them as when around with her would typically end in a fight. And Brian and the girls felt torn. Even though she wasn't as nice to them as she should be, she was still Taylor. She was still fun, creative, and someone who did everything possible to ensure that even though she and I weren't getting along, she had her group of people, even if it was manipulative, knowing when with her, they weren't with me.

Just as I was contemplating all the thoughts, my phone rang. I looked down seeing the name Lynell Beckstrom. In all my years of knowing her, she has never called me.

"Hello," I said.

"Hey," she replied. "What's going on?"

And then suddenly, I broke down. "Lynell, I have no idea why you chose to call me right now, but I'm having a really hard time and don't know if I can go on. I need help to get through this. I need to clear this financial blockage I'm carrying."

"Let's do a Rapid Eye session and clear some blockages," she said. "We can schedule one tomorrow."

"Thank you, Lynell, you're a Godsend!" I don't know how she knew to call, but something in the ether let her know. I will forever and eternally be grateful she chose to listen to spirit at that time. If she hadn't, I'm uncertain I'd still be here.

Following that appointment and call, I knew I needed to continue with my inner work. I reached out to a gifted healer I'd interviewed for my Quantal U series. Our session was a powerful series of breath work utilizing specific words and visualization, one that I've recreated and used for personal healing multiple times since.

I was starting to feel better.

One of the things I adhered to during the pandemic was I watched hardly any information news, TV, or podcasts. Over the last year, I'd probably watched a dozen or so videos, preferring instead to feel what was happening, as I knew most sources of information were false or they were unknowingly feeding false information.

I was comfortable watching Quantum Truths with JC Kay. For some reason, the things she talked about resonated with me. She seemed a gifted psychic, a pursuer of truth, and a compassionate humanitarian. Still, I've seen maybe six or seven of her now over 300 episodes, most of which were sent to me by a trusted friend.

On April 3rd, I sat down and watched the 111th episode of JC Kay, fitting as 111 in numerology is all about new beginnings, new *aha's*, or new enlightenment and awareness regarding oneself. She had connected with and asked several questions of the trees, a way she felt was unadulterated when going within and connecting to spirit, to finding answers and getting to the truth of what was happening.

At around 19:21 minutes, JC Kay asked, "Is Princess Diana Alive?

The answer was, "Yes. In the form of a woman, who lives by the ocean, on a calm beach in Florida. She is given sanctuary there and sheltered daily."

When JC Kay said these words, I had a bullet of energy hit me squarely in the gut with the immediate thought, "She's talking about me."

Wait, is she serious? Is she talking about me? Really?

I'd heard for months that Princess Diana wasn't dead and would be reappearing, but *me*?! I thought as several doubts, questions, and confusion came flooding in.

How was this possible? We were alive at the same time! And then I remembered Wayne Dyer saying in his book that he met one of his lives while they were both alive. Because we're multi-dimensional, we often have multiple lifetimes at the same time.

The thoughts kept coming and coming. I had no way of knowing if it was possible, but I knew a way to find out. I needed to connect.

I quickly set up my bathroom sanctuary, lit my candles, and lit my *palo santo* to clear the space.

Once clear and the warm shower running, I started my breathwork. In two, three, four, hold, two, three, four, and out through the mouth. As I breathed out, I'd visualize a bright, healing cord of light coming from my abdomen connecting to my higher self as I'd say, "I Am Unconditional Love."

Over and over, I'd repeat, breath in two, three, four, hold two, three, four, slow breath out, "I Am Unconditional Love." After what seemed like several minutes of repeating this over and over, my upper lip began to tingle. Minutes after that, my hands started as well. Suddenly I saw a blur and flood of several images that appeared as a gallery of pictures hanging on a wall. Instantly, I knew I was observing several of my past lives. Princess Diana was one of these images, Joan of Arc, and Jesus another. Oddly enough, though Jesus was there, I still didn't connect him as one of my past lives. I simply passed him off as support. I also saw myself as a 300-year-old monk.

After seeing these images, I felt and was shown that this lifetime, my lifetime, is *the* lifetime, an accumulation of perspectives from all lifetimes. This was the lifetime to bring all the experiences together, all the times I've tried and failed, or all the times I gained experience by succeeding in doing similar work and purpose; this was finally the lifetime.

I was then shown images that looked like a matrix of numbers and then shown an image of Neo (Keanu Reeves from *The Matrix*) within the matrix of numbers, followed by the distinct impression that I was here to learn and remember the manipulation and illusion of the false matrix we live under.

And I knew I was here to learn how to work within it. To learn how to transcend and transmute it.

I even saw myself flying.

This ebbed its way to images of the military, followed by an image of John F. Kennedy Jr. walking on the beach toward me. When he reached me, we gave each other the biggest hug. I asked if he was alive and whether we were supposed to work together in this lifetime.

The immediate answer was *yes!*

But there was nothing I was to do; he'd find me. I simply needed to stay positive and continue forward.

A couple of days later, I received an offer to get ten free minutes with an online psychic, and I wanted to ask more about the business partner.

"I'm hoping to know more about this business partner of mine," I said to her. "I'm not sure who he is or when he's going to get in touch."

"How do you *not* know who he is," she said. "He's all over your field. You have to know who he is."

"It's not my husband?" I replied.

"No, this is a business partner. And you, you are bigger than that. Wait, do you have a picture you can send me?" she said.

"No," I thought to myself, "this doesn't feel right." And then my ten minutes were up. I never did send her a picture and I never followed up.

We were down in the Keys several days later for a few days of family vacation. While there, I was walking around downtown and came to a store offering palm readings. I walked inside and quickly paid.

"What does she have to say," I thought to myself.

She took me back to an enclosed room and held my hands face-up, reading them.

"I'm supposed to have a business partner I've been hearing about. Is there anything you can tell me about him?" I asked her.

"He will find you," she said. "But it won't be for several months. Maybe in the fall."

I sighed in disappointment.

"And you should be careful who you tell about yourself, about who you are" she said, looking me squarely in the eyes. "It could be dangerous."

I looked at her, shocked, as I hadn't told her anything about myself, let alone what I'd been channeling or who I'd been.

I left her shop wishing I had more answers.

Chapter Seven

The next few months were up and down in emotion. On the one hand, I'd just learned something incredible about myself. I really did have a big mission. I really was going to do something big for humanity. This was often followed by two to three days of disappointment, doubt, and uncertainty. Often, I'd fall into what seemed like a major depression, feeling as if nothing was possible and nothing would happen. Was this even real? Was I crazy, or worse, one big ego making me into someone special? And how do I believe something like this?

I felt manic, and sometimes my family wondered it too.

Aside from that, I had no idea what I was supposed to do or how I was supposed to do it. I wondered whether I should get a stable job that brought consistent income as I felt more lost than ever about my job and current situation. It had to be getting better soon, right?

At the end of June, we were headed back to Idaho and Oregon for the summer, and I knew I could figure out the job situation there. My grandmother had just passed away and we were returning for her funeral and a week of Souls with Stamina. At the time, the plan was to return to Florida, find an actual house, and plant some roots.

Pulling into my parent's place at the end of June, I saw their driveway filled with cars. Mom was hosting a Tibetan bowl class with several gifted healers, including Tracy Gibbons, an intuitive, past-life regression specialist, and psychic protector.

In the days leading up to it, I saw multiple groupings of 1111s, clueing me in that something would be soon revealed. I felt certain I needed to speak further with Tracy.

We met in the large guest bedroom downstairs, where Brian and I were staying for the next few weeks. I sat on the bed, and Tracy sat in a chair at the foot of it.

The conversation lasted a couple of hours, with me telling her my experience in learning of Diana, feeling crazy, wanting confirmation, and having no clue what exactly I was to be doing.

After listening to my story Tracy looked at me and said, "You have been several famous people in your lifetimes," she said with knowing, "and your soul is ancient. You have been around since before the beginning of Earth's existence. And you are one of the archangels and siblings to Archangel Jofiel, Archangel Michael, and Jesus Christ, to name a few. But who you are, is for you to discover yourself." She said, just as the name Uriel came flooding in.

"Uriel is coming in," I said.

"I'd ponder on it," she responded. "It will come to you."

The next morning, at the moment of awakening, half awake and half still in the dream state, I was flooded with the name Jesus and the immediate thought and confirmation that I'd been him.

I then had the impression that my sister Windy was Archangel Uriel, meaning Windy had wings.

There it was again.

Was I him? I'd seen it now multiple times in different ways. Was it possible? If so, what does it mean?

The next day when I told Tracy what name and feeling immediately came to me when I woke; my entire body felt electric, from my head to my toes bringing all hairs to stand on end, another indicator I was hearing truth.

"I also believe Windy is Uriel", I said, causing Tracy's body to light up and stand on end.

More confirmation.

If synchronicities are truly a clue to what is, without a doubt, the Universe wanted me to know.

Throughout that day and several after, I received several more confirmations.

When I had an aura picture with Shay, an amazing clairvoyant who'd found her gift as an aura reader 30 years earlier, she saw Mary Magdalene, someone she'd not seen before in any of the 7 or 8 reads I'd had with her over the years. Interesting as Mary Magdelene was obviously a very important person in Jesus's life.

When talking with a friend about wanting to explore and travel the world (not discussing religion or Jesus), she responded that was how Jesus learned his teachings. He traveled all over, learning from Gurus and teachers in multiple places, from Bali to India, to Egypt.

I hadn't seen my brother Ken since we'd left for Florida, and when I returned home, I realized we had the same haircut.

"It's Jesùs," my sister-in-law said. "He looks just like Jesùs!" And the truth was, he did, and by extension, I did. We had the same hair, similar coloring, and look we'd seen in multiple pictures of Jesus, including the one in my parent's living room.

Two weeks later, at Souls with Stamina, the week-long empowerment retreat I attend and work at every summer, I was on the table receiving an energy balance from a wonderful couple named Chris and Melanie Shipley.

Chris was asking a series of questions and muscle-testing the answer, determining if there were any areas we needed to balance. One of the questions was whether I see myself as God sees me.

'Did God see me as Jesus?" I thought to myself.

Muscle test: Strong

"Wow, Chris said, I've never seen anyone test strong to that question. Most of us see ourselves as completely different than God sees us."

There were too many synchronicities to count.

I was uncertain about this new revelation.

It was sacrilegious, scandalous even.

And I was too imperfect. Jesus is someone whom 70% of the world looks to for guidance and help on their path to salvation. Though mistranslated, His teachings and principles have been taught throughout churches and religions around the world for the last 2000 years.

He was also born a miracle, born to a virgin (which by all accounts we know to be factually true). He was beyond a mere mortal, just in how he was born. In truth, his conception was planned and occurred as other births in history have also occurred, via a light conception process, one that Joseph was aware of and agreed to. You can read a great description of a light conception in a book called *Anna, Grandmother of Jesus: A Message of Wisdom and Love* by Claire Heartsong. Here the author has channeled Jesus' grandmother and mother to Mary, an impressive Essene who'd mastered the art of eternal youth and lived for hundreds of years both leading up to his birth and following his ascension.

A light conception is created using etheric seed and DNA, whereas most pregnancies are conceived when the parents have (intercourse), or a physical conception using physical DNA and seed. In Jesus's case, Joseph's etheric seed and DNA were used, meaning it was an etheric union, one where he was created from the etheric blueprint of his parents, not their physical. Each blueprint is perfect, the DNA untainted by the generations and millennia of trauma we undergo in each Earth life.

The biggest difference between a soul created physically in our 3D Earth plane vs. etherically and energetically is that the physical DNA and seed aren't pure, and the etheric seed and DNA are pure, untainted, and perfect. A person born under this type of conception forgoes bringing in the generational crap we all carry. The trauma and patterns that continue to play out through each generation until a family member says enough is enough and breaks it, a generational chain breaker.

My Mom was one, I'm one, and my husband Brian is one.

I believe Jesus was born without taking all that on. He, and by extension, I, or better said, our Oversoul, our higher self, chose and contracted to play that part in this 3D matrix. A matrix with multiple dimensions and realities. Ones we can access when understanding how to shift our frequency, allowing us to see.

Psychics and mediums do it all the time, shifting their frequency to accommodate other dimensions, whether that of one where ghosts hang out, or the dimension of the spirit world, where I believe we go before and after death to rest, recover, and prepare for our next life. Even within the spirit world, there are different levels and dimensions, dependent on our vibrational frequency, at the time of our death. The spiritual level we transition to following death directly correlates to our soul's vibrational frequency.

It's probably why religions often talk about layers of heaven, such as in the Mormon religion, where there is a Celestial, Telestial, and Terrestrial layers in addition to a hell. In their religion, however, only someone baptized and married in the temple can make it to the highest Celestial Kingdom, the only place God resides and where we all want to be.

Meaning that according to their beliefs, the only people allowed into the Celestial Kingdom are members of the Church of Jesus Christ of Latter Day Saints; regardless of one's soul frequency or spiritual level of attainment at the time of their death.

This idea used to infuriate me growing up in a Latter-Day Saints family. My grandfather, Doug Mairs, was anything but Mormon, though he never stood in my grandmother's way of raising her boys in the Church, something very important to her. Grandpa was one of the most honest, hardworking, and trustworthy men and businessmen I'd ever known. I grew up hearing the stories and would randomly meet people who, once they found out who I was, would regale me with stories or admiration of how amazing and honest a guy he was.

But he wasn't Mormon. And when he died, the idea he wouldn't be allowed in the Celestial Kingdom simply because he wasn't 'baptized and married in the temple' was frustrating. And yet he was more honest, trustworthy, and compassionate than most people. At the time of his death, I didn't believe God would disallow him access to a higher kingdom or level simply because he wasn't baptized.

Because he way I look at it, it doesn't matter if you were married in a sacred temple. It matters what you do with your life. It matters how you treat people, work with people, and give and offer service. Most importantly, it matters how you treat and love yourself. *That* is what matters at the end of the day. Those are the things people regret on their deathbeds.

I firmly believed my grandfather rivaled any God-fearing Latter-Day Saints man in honesty, service, integrity, heart, and compassion. All the principles and attributes suggestive of an advanced soul, someone my grandfather most certainly was.

For example, someone choosing to murder innocent people in their lifetime will have a significantly lower vibrational frequency at the time of their death than, say, Wayne Dyer at the time of his death. He was an incredible example of compassion, love, and generosity throughout his life. I remember hearing him speak about the time, on his birthday, when he took a couple of thousand dollars' worth of 100-dollar bills and started passing them out to everyone on the street, the homeless especially. Wayne Dyer was a walking, talking man of God. And you could feel it in his presence, how he spoke, and how he treated others. At the time of his death, his vibrational frequency was extremely high compared with someone learning the 3D life experience of being a murderer.

I also believe I am not the only Jesus, simply that my Oversoul was the Jesus in *this* reality. An avatar, born without the generational shit most of us bring with us at the time of our birth. And because he didn't deal with the extra baggage, his spiritual connection, understanding, and awareness were heightened compared to most, allowing an almost perfect-like understanding of the Universe, its laws, and how to master them. Jesus was brought into the world using spiritual technology and knowledge. In addition, he was raised as an Essene, being taught the skills of astral travel, bilocation, transcendence, and discerning between various energies and entities from a very young age. At the age of eight, he underwent his first initiation, a four-day, four-night ceremony, left alone at the top of Mt. Sinai. He was given no food, water, or shelter. There he communed with spirits, angels, demons, and even his parents, passing the time until the four days were over.

And though our OverSoul is ancient and more advanced, it's on the same evolutionary path as every other soul in the Universe. No different than anyone else.

That still didn't mean in my 3D world and brain that I truly believed it was possible. I had so many doubts, my confidence ebbed and flowed depending on the day.

I knew my heart was big and wanted to heal the world, but so many others want that as well.

I knew there were better ways to practice medicine and help others heal, as did others.

I have healing gifts, but so do others.

The idea was hard to wrap my head around. And because of the 'crazy' sounding nature of it, I really had no one I could speak to about it. A week or two after Souls with Stamina, I tried telling my Mom. I'm unsure what she believed or still believes, as we haven't spoken about it since that day.

At the end of Souls with Stamina, I sat down for a read with Lisa, a wonderful psychic and medium. I'd never had one before, and throughout the week, she would tell me various things she was *seeing*, such as the business partner. I, of course, wanted to know more.

I felt comfortable telling her what I learned about Princess Diana but nothing more as I wanted to see what she'd channel.

At first, we talked about Brian's Grandpa, helping him pass.

Then Lisa walked behind me and placed her hands on my shoulders to narrow in and focus.

Suddenly she looked up, exclaiming, "Oh my God, Oh my God, it's actually her, it's Princess Diana! She's so beautiful!"

"And she's rubbing your hair from behind."

"Oh my God, I can't believe she's actually here," Lisa exclaimed again, pure amazement in her voice.

"She says you have the heart of a warrior, the mind of a King. Actually, Queen, Diana is correcting me," Lisa said, laughing. "The mind of a Queen." She laughed again.

She's funny! And has as quite a sense of humor. Lisa exclaimed.

"I'm funny too!" I respond laughing. We must have that in common," I smile.

"She's saying the Obamas are not what they seem. Michele is really a man and their children obviously aren't theirs.

"She says this new vaccine is dangerous, and in a few years, there will be large numbers of infertility, complications, and other problems associated with it."

"Birth numbers are going to decline."

"Wait, she's crying so hard, I can hardly understand her. Can you please slow down?" Lisa asked.

"She says it's of utmost importance to tell as many people as possible. Write senators, congress, our politicians; any and everyone."

"By next year, you'll have 12 people working for you, and your business will begin to expand and grow."

"I keep seeing one too many, one voice too many," she said, gesturing with her hands.

"One too many."

When leaving Souls with Stamina, we intended to return to Florida, but too many things had changed. While tensions and the relationship with Taylor was still very difficult, our reason for not moving to Florida was a concern for her and her alone. While at Souls, Taylor was giving Lisa a hug when suddenly she pushed Taylor to arm's length looking deeply at her, as she'd just *seen* a vision of her in an accident.

In the vision, Lisa sees a headstone with Taylor's name and a crack running through it, indicating a near-death experience. She sees Taylor getting into the truck of a guy she knows. They have a physical altercation, causing a car accident and Taylor's near-death experience. Lisa describes the guy, his tattoo, his age, and the make and model of this truck.

Unbeknownst to Lisa, she described the *exact* guy Taylor worked with at Papa's Raw Bar, right up to his tattoo and license plate number. The same person Taylor had been coming home, talking and excited about.

That was the deciding factor. And while I had no idea whether Taylor would experience something similar anywhere else we lived, I knew we'd at least be close to family and would have their support if something did occur.

The Boise/Meridian, ID area was decided, and we soon started looking for a place to live. I had no idea how we'd guarantee to pay the monthly rent, but my family needed a place to land and call their own. Luckily, of the three rentals we visited, one was a great size and fit for our family, and we had no issues getting approval.

We moved in the weekend before school started, and other than a few mattresses, and a dresser or two, we had no bedroom or living room furniture, but at least it was our own place. Something we hadn't had for close to ten months.

The next three months were a whirlwind of emotional upheavals, from wondering whether we'd ever be a family of five again to wondering whether I'd finally be able to get my business up and going and start bringing in more consistent income. As soon as we left SWS, any behavior from Taylor that appeared to be making amends disappeared. She was furiously angry we were moving to Boise, the last place she wanted to be.

Trying to ensure the easiest transition for Bella and Taylor, we enrolled them in the brand-new high school in Meridian, ID, named Owyhee. I figured they'd be new kids, but so would everyone else. And I signed them up to join a local studio competition team, where they already had close dance friends with whom they used to travel and dance every summer for weeks at a time. At the very least, I figured the girls would be at a studio with friends and a supportive start.

Most importantly, it offered their only consistent activity through everything. Through all the moves and the pandemic.

For Taylor especially, I knew dance was an important expression of catharsis and a way to work through difficult emotions.

If there was nothing else I could promise or do for her, at the very least, we'd have her in a strong, supportive dance environment.

And regardless of anything else, I'd figure out how to pay for it, come high or hell water.

Unfortunately, how wrong I was.

From the first day Taylor walked into her new studio, she felt unwanted. The girls she thought would take her in and include her didn't, barely glancing her way or saying hello. This was devastating for her as dance had always been a respite and break from the chaos of life. And now she started to dread going, soon having anxiety and crying spells.

School was not going well either. By nature, Taylor is and has always been a straight-A student, but after 4 - 6 weeks, we found her failing or had D's in several classes. Unbeknownst to me, she was also skipping, often dealing with anxiety in the bathroom or leaving school altogether. On top of everything, she was self-sabotaging. One morning we found her in bed with a random guy. In addition, she was drinking and partying. It felt like a matter of time before something major occurred. Whenever we tried to punish her, such as taking away her phone or other privileges, she'd refuse to obey or buy herself a burner phone. The only way to make her do anything would've been through physical force, something Brian and I weren't OK doing.

If we'd taken her for medical treatment, she'd have been diagnosed with oppositional defiant disorder. This disorder typically sees little improvement with either medication or therapy, usually leading to a diagnosis of borderline personality by the time they're an adult, often finding them in and out of jail throughout their life.

At the beginning of October, Taylor had to meet with her school counselor as she'd gotten in trouble when the school cop found paraphernalia, a pipe, in the car she was driving. It wasn't her paraphernalia (as she was driving her uncle's car to school that day, which he'd dropped off the night before.) Bella and a couple of other friends were in the car at lunch when the cop saw them and began searching the car as he noted smelling something (denied by all the girls). In his search, he discovered a small pipe with nothing in it.

Because the school had a no-tolerance policy, and Taylor was the one who drove the car, she was punished, which was why she was meeting with the counselor.

The information revealed in that counseling session was concerning. She'd suffered a sexual assault a year prior, and I never knew. Add that to her current mood and actions, and I was actively worried she might harm herself, which

Taylor thought possible as well. She began to talk about not wanting to be here, hating life, and wanting it to end.

Feeling desperate, I knew she needed help. At the end of October, I'd been planning a *woo-woo* weekend with my husband, Mom, and several healers in the community, including Tracy, the person who confirmed and added to everything I'd recently channeled. Not only is she a gifted intuit and past-life specialist, but she also helps psychically clear negative energies and entities from other persons' energy fields, their houses, or other spaces needing to be cleared.

I felt Taylor should come as well. The nature of our relationship was that I'd have to bribe her, which I did, offering to give her phone back weeks before she was supposed to have it back.

To say the weekend was one of the most profound in my family's lives is an understatement.

I only hope to give the experience the justice it deserves.

We arrived at the cabin in Utah Friday evening. It wasn't until the next morning that I asked Tracy if she would take a *look* and see if negative entities or energies were attached to her.

"Is she willing to let me work on her?" Tracy asked.

"Yes," I said. "She told me she was."

"OK," she replied. "I'll see if anything presents itself." She went back to her conversation.

Approximately 30 minutes later, Tracy started playing a Tibetan bowl and instructed some of the others skilled in bowl and chime therapy to join in. She then walked over to Taylor, looked directly at her, and asked, "Is it OK if I work on you?"

"Yes," Taylor replied, somewhat hesitantly.

"OK, we're going to play some music. Would you be willing to stand in this bowl here?" she asked, directing her attention to a large Tibetan bowl, approximately 2-3 feet wide in diameter.

"Sure," she replied, looking more and more like she wanted to run.

"You may feel weak and possibly like you may fall. It's OK, we're all here, and we'll catch you," Tracy responded.

She beckoned me to support one side of the bowl as Taylor stepped into it.

Music, chimes, and bowls ringing in harmony between all those playing.

I'm not sure about the space of time or how long Taylor stood in the bowl, maybe 5 - 10 minutes. But suddenly, she fell forward, and Tracy caught her, leaned over and whispered something in her ear, then said loudly to her partner, "Royce, get it now."

He swept in, grabbed at the *air* over Taylor's back, yanked at something, and threw it over to Archangel Michael to dispose of.

Taylor immediately heaved forward, then completely collapsed, sobbing, where she stayed for several minutes.

When she was finally able to get up, I was initially uncertain anything had actually occurred, as she was still very reserved, cool, and standoffish with me, her normal mood whenever I was around.

Later that night, after everyone went to bed, I was left downstairs with Tracy, Brian, and Taylor. Suddenly, Tracy looked at Taylor and said, "You have choice, you know. You'll always have choice. You can choose to accept the shift and changes that occurred here earlier today or you can opt in to the life you were headed for. That entity was dirty, nasty, and gross. It wanted you to think horrible things about yourself, but especially your Mom. Because she is so strong and powerful, it wanted to destroy her. And it wanted to destroy your confidence. But you have running within you the power of Joan of Arc and many other powerful warriors. And you have a purpose in this life, but you will have to choose."

Suddenly I saw in my mind the powerful presence of an Angel entering the room. I saw the wings spread from one end of the great room to the other, as if in a hug embrace.

And I knew just as instantaneously it was Windy.

Exactly at the same time, Tracy said, "Your Aunt Windy is here. Can you feel her? She wants you to know she is with you and has always been with you. In fact, part of the reason she left was to help assist *you* on the other side. As she knew this would be a very difficult time. She loves you and will be with you for the next several months to help you energetically acclimate and transition from the weight the entity wrapped you in."

I was sobbing and crying. This was the first ray of hope we'd seen in years of being the cohesive family we'd once been.

And I was over the moon.

Three weeks later, we were sitting around our Thanksgiving table. As tradition goes, we make the rounds, sharing our gratitude and thanks with others. For almost four years, I'd barely heard Taylor utter the words, "I love you." Never with regular consistency and most certainly not of her own volition.

As it came to her turn, she looked straight into my eyes and said, "I'm grateful to Mom, for never giving up, and for doing everything possible to find the answer, at a time when it felt like there was a foot pressed to my neck, pushing me further into the ground. Thank you for loving and never giving up on me. I love you," she said.

I was bawling.

In that moment, I realized that 2021 was one of the most important and influential years for my family, for which I am eternally grateful.

Chapter Eight

Optimistic about expanding my practice to one that included Reiki, cranial sacral, and bodywork, I began working to make that happen, increasing my skills as a healer, in-person and virtually. I wanted to become more confident with distance sessions (as distance makes absolutely no difference when tapping into the zero-point field).

At this time, the delta variant was beginning to pick up speed, and I saw more and more people with Covid. I also began seeing more posts on social media about family members, friends, or loved ones in the hospital needing intubation, and many of them dying. Through my business, I was prescribing medication to help with the acute infection. I also began offering Reiki, medical consultations, and the AO frequency scanner to help.

At any given time, our bodies emit over 120,000 different frequencies or energetic wavelengths relating to every cell, every hormone level, every muscle fiber or each and every lab test which the AO frequency scanner is able to pick up. And much like an episode of Star Trek, we now have the technology and capability to energetically scan and measure thyroid levels, cholesterol, inflammatory markers, kidney, liver and brain function, allergies or food/pollen sensitivities, whether our chakra or meridian systems are open, and more.

The AO frequency scanner was created with the same quantum technology as discovered by Tesla and used by the Russian cosmonaut space program, allowing them to keep track of their astronauts' vitals, potential illnesses, and overall health. Utilizing bio resonance technology, the AO scanner picks up on tissue and hormone abnormalities of a person based off the frequency they're emitting.

It then helps balance the person energetically with specific tones, music, or notes that specifically target the areas of blockage and congestion.

Think about a radio station that when you turn the dial 1-2 clicks any direction, you can still hear the station, though there's static in the way. This is similar to what happens with our own frequencies when they've had interference from destructive frequencies or wavelengths within our Field and environment. When we're blocked, we're out of flow, not in energetic balance, and our physical body feels the effects.

Thankfully, the AO scanner helps to detect and open these blockages.

While scrolling on social media one day, I noted that a friend mentioned her Dad being in the hospital for Covid, and she was very concerned. A couple of days later, I saw another post about him, as he didn't seem to be improving, and there was fear he'd become intubated. After seeing this, I intuitively felt I should reach out and ask if it would be OK to work on him.

She agreed.

The next morning in my shower, I spent the next 30+ minutes clearing his energy field of the virus, removing any dark areas I found in his head and chest, and replacing them with pure, healing light.

When I got out, I texted Ashley, telling her I'd just worked on him and explaining a little of what I saw.

She immediately texted me back, "Oh my goodness Elisa, can you tell me what time you did this? I only ask because I literally JUST got off the phone with him seconds ago, and he sounded so different I cried the whole time. The doctors said his mind is clearer today than it's been in ten days. He actually knew what day it was and could connect his thoughts to me (which hasn't happened in a week!) I talked to him about continuing to fight for us, and he said, "I've never not wanted to fight. You guys are everything I'm fighting for. I just didn't know if I could keep fighting...but right now, it feels like I can." I'm literally floored right now and in tears."

I couldn't believe it. What an incredible experience.

Overnight his oxygen requirement dropped another 30% and he was released home the following day.

Throughout the fall and into January, I continued offering and doing similar distance healings with good results. I loved this aspect of using the Field, even when thousands of miles away.

In addition, I became involved in and began speaking out on my concerns for the new Covid vaccine now becoming mandated for hospitals, healthcare systems, and other businesses around the country.

Like so many others, I was shocked at what I saw as concerning data and the apparent blindness of so many of my medical colleagues. Never in the history of my medical career had I seen so many excited to jump on the wagon of "we're following the science" when it was very clearly *not* science.

Two months of study is never science.

And to see the mass insistence which so many colleagues adopted in pushing an unscientific shot at our most vulnerable was shocking.

Especially when I'd experienced *years* of training, hounding us about the concerns of taking anything in the first trimester, even cautioning the use of medicine as simple as Tylenol.

And yet, for some unbelievable reason, we were fine giving it to everyone.

But I soon started seeing people with injuries to the vaccine and started seeing suspicious and correlated diseases pop up.

In all my years of medicine, I'd seen only a handful of vaccine injuries, most of these in younger women presenting with POTS (postural orthostatic tachycardia syndrome) causing low blood pressure, a fast heart rate, dizziness and fatigue and/or other debilitating neurological diseases such as acute flaccid paralysis. My first experience was in residency caring for a woman who developed Guillan Barre Syndrome from her flu shot. After several months in the ICU, we finally sent her to a nursing home, with a tracheotomy in place to help her breathe. Not long after, she returned to the ICU with difficulty breathing and soon after passed away. She was only in her forties.

Another patient was a young girl, 17 years old. She came to see me after a 3-month stint of flaccid paralysis where she could not walk, followed by severe POTS that she still deals with daily several years later. The symptoms started three days after she received three vaccines needed to attend college in the fall. Interestingly she was only to receive two, the flu shot and her meningococcal vaccine, as she did not want the HPV.

However, according to her, they gave her three, though there is no documentation of the third shot.

I've seen severe myositis of the deltoid muscle three times, causing months and, for some, years of pain, surgery, and physical therapy needed to recover from it. One staff member was out for four months, recovering from the surgery she required following her flu shot, the effects of which still impact her day-to-day quality of life.

I watched as a 20-year kidney plant recipient fell ill for 4 - 6 weeks every year after her flu shot. She felt terrible, but her nephrologist kept insisting she take it. She finally asked my opinion, and I told her I didn't feel she should have it this year. In my mind, it was wreaking havoc on her immune system and severely decreasing her quality of life. Two months later, she returned, reporting how good her health had been and remarking on one of the best holidays she'd had, as it was the first time, she hadn't been sick during Christmas in several years.

I saw these injuries over approximately 8 - 10 years, but in a matter of several months, I suddenly saw multiple injuries in people following their Covid vaccine.

For some, it was major, as in the case of a lady I interviewed, who, three days after her shot, experienced severe eye pain (discovered as a stroke and eventually leading to blindness) and severe neurological problems so severe she had to quit working. For the next two years, her health continued to struggle and decline until she succumbed to her injuries and passed away in January of 2023.

For others, the side effects were less but still interfering. Healthy women athletes suddenly experiencing chest pain and tightness following their shots, along with menstrual changes or unexpected miscarriages and stillbirths. I began seeing and hearing about heart attacks in younger men and descriptions of blood clots that didn't fit the typical picture.

In the last two years, I can count multiple friends and family members who've had weird and unusual events or situations. My young, healthy brother had a massive stroke, and another healthy friend had a heart attack. I've watched as another friend, and her entire extended family, suffered from Covid illness after Covid illness, along with multiple other illnesses and problems such as recurrent illness, new or worsening heart problems, inflammatory reactions, and kidney infections, just to name a few.

Another lady came to see me after her first booster shot, whereby, soon after, she began having worsening abdominal pain, and her arthritic knee pain intensified to the point of unbearable.

And it didn't matter. Regardless of the three Covid shots she took to protect herself; she still came down with Covid two months later, causing multiple trips to the hospital and taking several weeks to finally heal.

Worst of all were all the new cancers I saw popping up in a matter of months. Cancers in young, healthy kids and adults. Cancers screened for months earlier, where nothing was found.

The injuries were coming from all over...how was it possible so many of my colleagues were still too blind to see?

Even the reporting system was showing reports of injuries that were increasing by leaps and bounds, and yet mainstream media (MSM) continued to push the narrative those reports didn't mean anything. Deaths jumped to 20,000 in a matter of months, then suddenly crept to a crawl, though continued to climb. Total injuries were soon reported at over a million, an increase to the reporting system by 1001%.

How in the hell was it possible so many of my colleagues couldn't and refused to see? Or, at the very least, start to ask questions.

Instead of touting, "Correlation doesn't mean causation."

It soon became obvious there was something wrong, intentional divisions to keep us in fear, divided, and fighting.

This, to me, was not a coincidence, confirming once again the intentional foul play underfoot. We weren't just dealing with a virus. This was a spiritual war against the forces of dark and evil. Against those entities and energies wishing us emotional pain, living off our low, dark, heavy emotions they call *loosh*, which is their food.

Because of this and my ongoing concerns regarding the vaccine, I began to actively promote and write medical exemptions for people, using any and all data I could find. Much of it came from data and studies from other countries. For some reason, the US had very little, if any, good data.

Another mind-boggling head-scratcher: We're in the middle of a pandemic, with a virus that is supposedly wreaking havoc across the globe, and we put out a treatment (I refuse to call it a vaccine) that is mandated without study completion. What is the next best thing to do to ensure the safety we keep telling people is there?

In my mind, the answer is very simple. We track and monitor each and every individual who receives the vaccine. Easy to do, especially as 99% of all medical systems are EMR and have easy built-in systems to add the tracking with reminders for follow-up.

But for some reason, this was never done.

And, the studies or data we did have were typically poor in that they lacked participant numbers, length of study time, or completely left out information to intentionally change the study outcome.

It was obvious. Not only was there corruption with the virus itself but there was also corruption and an ulterior motive with this vaccine. Everything in my body was screaming that it wasn't safe or good for our health or humanity.

Suddenly multiple videos and stories of those injured were wiped out, covered up, or censored. I began hearing stories from individuals unable to tell their experiences. At the same time, most social media platforms and MSM continued to promote vaccine safety and efficacy stories.

As I was so vocal, I quickly found the majority of my medical colleagues were turning their back on me, even those in my spiritual and *woo-woo* physician groups. These were the ones who believed in the multi-dimensional aspect of us and understood the importance of trauma and emotional healing. Many of them were medical intuitives, psychics, and other healers utilizing energy work in their own practices. I thought for sure the majority of them would have my back and ring support, forming a group of physician truthers. For surely, if they're this spiritual, they've done the work to know this injection wasn't created through the right process. And surely, they had to know everything happening is part of a much bigger spiritual warfare, which has been talked about and promised for centuries.

Unfortunately, except for two or three physicians who reached out, offering their support via messenger, the rest of the women in this group turned their backs. Either not believing what I was saying and/or drinking the Kool-Aid themselves.

At some point in early 2021, I joined an email group of physicians, epidemiologists, biologists, lawyers, and more, from all over the world. It was wonderful and confirming to read and hear what I'd been feeling, knowing, and seeing myself they were feeling and knowing as well.

Aside from this group, I felt completely and utterly alone in the medical and professional world. And in some cases, in my personal one as well.

In my extended family, though ½ of them chose to receive the injection, there was no discord or unwillingness to see and hang out together. We felt each person was free to choose, and though several of us were concerned for others, we continued to love and support them the same.

Not the case for other family members and friends, as so many others have experienced.

The worst for us was not being invited to Thanksgiving with family we'd felt the closest to (of all Brian's extended family) before the pandemic. We hadn't received the vaccine, and they needed to protect their children from us. It's now been over three years since we've seen them, one family living very close to us here in Boise.

My girls were extremely hurt by this, especially as my viewpoint was that every time we hung around those who've been vaccinated, especially recently vaccinated, we ran the risk of catching Covid via a process called shedding. It had already happened to my daughter Emi after inviting a friend over who'd been vaccinated the same day.

As soon her friend got into the car, remarking on her sore arm, I instantly knew Emi would most likely get it.

Sure enough, when they woke the next day, her friend complained of a headache, mild fever, achy body, and a sore arm.

By that night, Emi began exhibiting the same symptoms, the next day feeling the worst with a fever. By Tuesday, she was feeling much better, but once again, I received confirmation this injection was not safe and certainly wasn't preventing transmission.

Along with medical exemptions, I worked on promoting my in-person business. To save money, as we couldn't afford a commercial space, I was seeing people out of my home and/or seeing them virtually. I also started a telehealth business to help people while sick with Covid. I once again felt like we were moving in the right direction. Something was finally happening.

By the end of December, my telehealth business had come to a crawl, and I was writing fewer exemptions. Once again, I was faced with a concern for our finances. I had thought my telehealth and in-person business would continue to grow, but it didn't seem to be the case. My marketing was limited to what I put on my personal page on Facebook, my business page on Instagram, and the few hundred or so I have on my email list. I didn't have the money for marketing and certainly wasn't going to borrow it. And with shadow banning, it wouldn't have mattered.

I also didn't take insurance, as they're incredibly corrupt, so essentially was running a concierge service, making it difficult to grow a medical business.

The pattern of financial lack continued to repeat itself. It was devastating, confidence-shattering, and made it very difficult to trust anything good would soon be happening. I knew my thoughts had a big impact and I would do everything I could to ensure we had the money we needed in our account. The problem was I couldn't ever guarantee consistent income, whether from Brian or myself. I was desperate for some financial stability every month.

The way it was now, we had none.

The way it was now, we couldn't plan or budget, as we had no idea what we'd have available to budget for.

Hoping for answers and to figure out my next best step, I sought help.

Chapter Nine

In January, I booked an appointment with an internationally known psychic, Bonnie McCliss. I had met her a year earlier when she interviewed me for her podcast, *Unworldly Everything* and we'd kept in touch. In fact, she had graciously led a Psychic Intuitive class, at no cost, for me and another physician several months earlier.

Skilled in Akashic records work with hypnotherapy, mediumship, and psychic abilities; each session differs depending on the client's wants and needs. Connected to and stored within the Field, our Akashic records are a recording and compilation of every moment in history, every future event, and each thought, emotion, intent, or words said in the history of our Universe. They hold the knowledge and information regarding every past, present, or future lifetime of each and every entity and life form; not just humans.

I wanted to know what I needed to do to finally get past my pattern of financial lack and learn more about my life's mission. I didn't mind the hard work and, at that point, knew I was in a loop of repeating the same pattern and thoughts, keeping me stuck in lack. And though I'd done tons of work on this specifically, like an onion, there is always additional work we need to do as the layers pull away.

But I was frustrated, as all the things I'd been told would come to pass hadn't. It felt like the worst assault ever and worst of all, I was losing trust in everything. As much as I wanted to believe, the lack of anything happening kept me feeling crazy and untrusting that anything would change. And, of course, it left me untrusting myself, untrusting what I'd channeled and what I'd been told.

How did I know this wasn't just my grand imagination?

I felt hopeless about our situation and realized I was also missing or suppressing my own magnetism. My magnetism in drawing people in wasn't there, or at the very least, severely lacking. In addition, we had little money to spend on anything beyond the essentials, I needed help, and I needed it now.

And, because I wanted a complete non-biased, and authentic reading, I didn't tell Bonnie anything I'd channeled about myself.

What's written next are parts of the transcribed sessions I recorded.

Bonnie

Hello!

Bonnie's voice rang loudly.

Bonnie

Elisa, how are you doing?

Elisa

Definitely felt things shifted after our last session. And there's been a lot of stuff I've been diving into. Where is this supposed to go? I've been feeling very impressed I need to start seeing people in person.

Elisa

I would love some clarification on whether to plan a retreat. Where I struggle is trusting me.

Bonnie

So, you'd like me to help analyze and figure out where you might be bottle-necking?

Elisa

Yes, coming into the appointment, I want whatever is needed for my highest and best.

Bonnie

Perfect! So when you say I want clarification, on kind of my journey, in regards to my teaching, and you are struggling a lot with the trusting.

Elisa

Yes, I invested a lot of time and money into similar ideas, and they never came together. I feel I need to trust that it is going to happen. But I just want to know, is this going to be a flop again?

The fear and doubt were evident in my voice.

Bonnie

That's kind of what I'm getting. OK, so let's start with the hard truth. A couple of different things. You are absolutely going to be successful with this, Elisa, and I'm not just telling you that because it's what you want to hear, it's evidential. Uh, as far as the way psychic stuff comes together. It's going to go far and wide. And I'm sure of that. Um, your soul is sure of that. And I think what throws you for a loop is that you psychically and intuitively know that that's going to be the truth, but it's not physically manifesting or hasn't yet. So, it's giving you, almost what we call a shattering, or this, it's the worst thing possible, honestly, this "I can't trust myself." It's almost like we have a divorce with our own intuition. You got all the stuff, you implemented it, and didn't get to where you were going. So, all this stuff you had faith in, as far as manifestation, creation, and forging ahead, and then not having evidential things to show for it, for lack of a better word, by what your standards are, um, is kind of heartbreaking.

Bonnie

So, the first thing, um, again, it is going to be radically successful. I feel that you're coming out of deep sadness around this and grief.

Elisa

Yeah, I've had a lot of trauma with this.

My voice broke, and sobs were evident.

Bonnie(her voice softened)

Yeah, I feel that.

Elisa

And I am totally aware of it. It was really devastating because I put everything into what I thought I was supposed to be doing. You know.

Bonnie

You weren't wrong, Elisa, you weren't wrong. You didn't actually fail at any point. So, what we do know is there is grief, and there is heartbreak, and we have to honor that because if we skip that step, we're going off track, OK?

Um, so then, the next question is, well, honoring it. And oh, I feel you. When you get into that, like good God, love you, I can feel that pain that you carry.

So, then we carry it to this map. The map is the shape of a spiral, where nothing makes sense in your mind as it's linear.

There's something happening to you in the negative space of what you perceive as failure, or failure to launch, or whatever, or not going. It's very necessary for where you're going. So, this failure to launch is part of what needs to happen to get it to work.

And I'm going to tell you where we are and where we need to go to not perpetuate pain.

It's kind of like digging out a well.

You're excavating really deep space as the channel. One of the most important things about you, Elisa, is your ability to touch higher worlds, other dimensions, information, signs, and knowledge. That's more important than anything. And I know, it's like, "No, I need to feed my family." God knows I've been there. But that becomes a huge part of the process of what you want to achieve by going forward in all this.

Elisa

Yeah.

Bonnie

So, something, two things are going on simultaneously, a consciousness shift, a damn death, and I wrote it down, she's going through a death, she's going through a death, and unwinding, so you can become this conduit for information, OK?

OK, and a journey forward.

So, here's my point, if I can bring it all together: If you can start to see that the failure has been a part of the divine refinement of you as a channel.

Not like in making you humble. That isn't what Bonnie is saying. Shifting neurobiology, the little billions of neurons in your head are being calibrated differently because of this.

Your heart is deep, wounded, expanded, and broken because of this.

And you are highly advised. You have very high guides, Elisa. And so, it's like if you can get to a place, this is the part of the delivery system that's going to make this very successful, believe that or not, you can start to shed layers of this wounded grief. We don't need hypnosis. We just need reconciliation of what the hell, why is this happening, and where is this helpful.

Elisa

Right.

Bonnie

You know, you told me to do this. Why is it not working? Like, what the hell? You know?

Elisa

Right.

Bonnie

I want to talk about one more philosophical agent with all of this.

There is a pain also, more of a personal pain.

We know that the cycles of your creation are divine, and something is up that we can't see in the here and now.

But your personal pain, I think, is maybe, but I'm not going to spend a lot of time on this, Elisa, because it's confusing, more going to talk about how to solve it, but I think it might be generational, but there's a "see me, see me, do you see me? Do you see me?" It's not ego. It comes from a heart place. I want to help and heal. But it's like this pain of invisibility. I'm right here, I'm talking, I'm doing my work.

Elisa

(thinking to myself)

The magnetism.

Bonnie

This is a hard one to get. It's actually power vs. force. And this is about the dynamics of energy. And I'm going to teach you about that, instinctively, somewhere deep inside of you, in some unconscious realm, you're putting power outside of you, projecting, pushing it out. See it, people, get it, people, respond, people. Give back to me so I can give back to you, turn that wheel of reciprocity.

It should be the exact opposite of what you're doing. You're putting a lot of force and power outside of you, but what we want to try and do is make you a magnetic force.

Elisa

Yeah, I want people to be drawn to me.

Bonnie

Yes, but energetically, you're doing the exact opposite. You need to flip the energy, and so I think first is reconciling grief and saying, "OK, I love you, I forgive you, I don't understand it, but I can believe this is for a bigger purpose, so this is an accumulative thing that I've going to choose to have faith and move forward, instead of all these multiple losses."

The second thing is external vs. internal power. We need to let go of external power. Now let me give you an example of that. I like what you're doing with the in-person. We need to get your money, and we need to showcase what you can do for the individual. That is your priority. As far as I can see.

You talk about, "Do I just need to get a job?" God love you. You are in so much pain. I mean, I can feel where you've dropped a lot of it, just in reading you now.

This in-person tactile energy is the best thing you have to offer right now.

That's what you're going to feed home base. Doing whatever you can do to get them into the 9 to 5 physically will buy you time.

But as successful as it will be, I don't believe the retreat idea is the best right now. Because you're trying to give it out before it's integrated into yourself fully.

I'd rather you write, not Zoom.

Let it percolate a little bit more. And in that way, you hold, and refine.

Write. Write, Elisa. I'd rather you put out a book right now, I'd rather you put a book out.

Because we want you to keep the information, percolate in it.

This is an internal power you are cultivating, the depth. Go back to that visual of culling out the well. We're going deeper and deeper. And every time you hold this, you'll have to deal with it. Am I going to get left behind? Will people see me? Am I going to miss my mark? That's primal, Elisa. That's old.

You will not get left behind, Elisa, I swear to you, um, but I think what you need is a deeper meditative conscious awareness. We want to stabilize you as a channel.

You have to get to that place where you're not only trusting yourself as a channel, but you can also play around with the exchange of information, From a higher dimension.

If you don't do that first, you're still doing the external power thing. That's weak.

It's like, see me! See me! Get this! But you haven't procured or strengthened the beacon or the magnet for people to say, I don't care what the hell you're selling; I want it.

It's the zero-point field, Elisa.

You are the carrier of the truth of zero-point energy. The zero-point field suggests that there is subatomic friction, or movement, that is moving and creating energy in a neutral, cool-down stage.

And it carries so much propulsion, it can blow up the damn planet, OK!

You will teach about zero-point. Go listen to Lynn McTaggart. She can put this in layman's terms. You have to be able to hold that. Yay!!

Elisa

Yeah.

Bonnie

Let's take a pause and see if this makes sense. You're getting all these psychic hits of what you're going to be doing, and you're implementing it too fast before you've secured and stabilized your inner core.

Elisa

Yeah, I just feel like everything has to be rushed. It has to be done. Like everything needs to happen right now. And also, behind that, I need to take care of my family.

Bonnie

I hear you; I hear you.

Listen, listen. And God knows I know what I'm telling you is accurate. You're picking up on two signals simultaneously. Your fear signal, you've got it, I've got it, we all have it. But you're also picking up on, I'm going to call it your Alien signal. When someone is tapped into higher teachers, God knows you are. We can keep going into that if you like, but they, it's velocity. In their energetic message, in the form of resonance, vibration, and mathematics. It hits your neural processing center, and it hits at a Richter scale of 10, which goes into the lower polyvagal and immediate fight or flight. And the message, when it comes through the brain mechanics, they're giving you an intense, "We need you, we need you now!"

But the *now* is in the form of an era, in the form of a coming of age. The way the brain reads it is wholly cow. I need to have this by Tuesday.

The era and message are now, it's very intense. But, the now is for this era. Listen to this. I'll get you there.

Give yourself a few more months. Pull yourself back. Get into a deep meditation practice.

You can feed your family because what we're cultivating is a magnetism, a magnetism where people will just find you.

Again, I don't care what you're selling. I don't know what you do, privatization. Private, private, private, private. They want you for themselves.

And in the meantime, after you've fed your family, and your bills are not haunting you, which is a priority, Elisa. If you cannot get ahead of the fear, what the hell else good is anything else? Forget about it. Take care of yourself first. Your family comes first. End of story, your family comes first. You and your family come first.

Then, you know, that's, you know, your bills and your money, you know, your stability.

Then comes your spiritual awareness, your consciousness. Your ability to trust yourself. Nothing else matters. This is the order of operations.

Then I can see you getting into deep meditative practices, and we can talk about what that looks like.

Doing it every day to the point that you're like, I don't care that I'm successful, because this is more fun.

She laughs.

Bonnie

Deep meditative practices. And what's going to happen to you is you're like, eh, retreat this, retreat that, it could happen, or it could not happen.

We need you to get to that point where you're so in this place of almost autonomy, Elisa.

That you're strong, that you're skipping steps in strength. You know, you have the knowledge. I'm not worried about your knowledge. It's your energetic strength, magnetism, and your pull, draw, and sustainability.

Elisa

Yeah.

Bonnie

If you do this, people will be begging for content. You will not have to beg them. If you do this, and if you don't, time expands until we get it right.

We need to get your spiritual, energetic body firing first. The knowledge is not the problem.

Long pause. Sobs are heard.

Elisa

I just want to do everything right, you know?

Bonnie(She whispers this back, her voice softening.)

I know.

Elisa

I want to fulfill my purpose. I want to help all the people I promised I would help. I feel such a pull for that.

Bonnie

I know.

Elisa

And um, I don't want to miss anything, I don't want to mess up, and, and, and, miss an opportunity because I was in my fear, in my shit, its, its...

Bonnie

You won't, Elisa. It's not possible. You're going to get this whether you suffer through and get it or you go through the stages of samadhi. OK, you will not. But this primal fear of being left behind is a thing, or failing the masses, it's a thing because of who you are, because of other timelines you've been associated with, whether it be the Atlantean times, we don't have to get into all that, you are a very intelligent woman who is feeling the collective of "Please don't let this timeline fail."

I don't know who you trust, Elisa, I don't know who's in that bracket of trust, but I feel you wouldn't call me if you didn't trust me, and I feel very capable of getting you to where you need to go, but I promise you're not going to get left behind, you're not going to fail anyone. When I tune in to you, your energy is kind of jumbled because you're trying to do 15 things at once. I know that place.

Bonnie

Doing that, you'll chase your tail. It doesn't go anywhere. And when you deliver to the masses, there's a hole in the bucket. You are designed to teach to the masses, to hundreds of thousands, if not millions of people, Elisa. You have to be able to speak with such electricity and force that they're taking in your light, not your knowledge. You're in light training right now, and so this is where I will not steer you wrong. We need you to become an ascetic, you know, the disciplined disciple of meditation, and the way I feel people can get through this is a strong faith. I don't know where you land in the world of faith.

Elisa

Yeah.

Bonnie

I don't know if you know your God. What does that look like for you? Where do you land?

Elisa

Yeah, Source, God, the Universe, whatever you call it, there is a direct central power that is energetically connected to all of us. And it is interwoven in between everything, its Spirit, the force between everything. The energy between all the matter.

Bonnie

You said things as talking about moments when you 'felt' God. Can you, when you touch God, what happens to you?

Elisa

I feel it in my body.

Bonnie

When?

Elisa

During shower meditations or binaural beats, then I go in, and I get to a point where I center myself and get into my heart space.

Elisa

And I ask, I'd love to feel you right now.

Elisa

Then I'd connect with my higher self or guides because I want to feel them.

Bonnie

I think you're grieving home. You're craving this connection.

Elisa

Yeah, I could sit for hours in meditation to be in that space and to feel and touch.

Bonnie

OK, OK. I think we can get you there.

If you were to have a real connective experience in the shower, when you're in it, you're in it, you're in it. Those are the days that fear won't win when you can be the channel you need to be.

Bonnie

I bet on the days you haven't given yourself the time to find this connection, I'll bet that's the time the fear comes in, and you're running around in chaos.

Elisa

Yep.

Bonnie

So, we know there's something about your connection that is the most important thing.

I think instead of processing your pain, you're trying to push away the pain by replacing it quickly.

Get into the shower and feel what you are feeling If it's enough to pull your molecules, let it happen. Feel that. Allow it to pass.

You have to allow it to happen and grieve it out. It will take more than a week. Let it out. You keep resetting.

You don't have to figure out how to heal the masses. That comes naturally. You don't have to figure out how to not leave anybody behind or fail them. That's the wrong focus.

You have to figure out, to export the grief that you hold and then hold the energetic high state through your practices and your mindfulness.

Elisa

Yeah, I know that I've been an Essene, their lifestyle, the depths of how they were connected, their entire life. Doesn't that sound incredible to do that every day? You're connected all the time. It brings me to tears; it's that powerful. I want to experience it every day.

Bonnie

And that's it; it's the deepening of your well through the pains you've been through when you're like, "I did it, it didn't work, I'm a failure to launch."

I know it sounds confusing. This is the part of you working out the mortal wound of grief because you're not in what you just described.

You've been working out the fall of man, kind of like your own fall of separation. Of, from the Essenes, from God. This primal separation from family.

So, you know, let's see if I can make this really clear.

I know you know this in your brain, but I don't think you're doing it electrically because I just feel you're not. It's the magnetism.

Elisa

I know a few of the people, who were in my past lives, and their magnetism...is amazing. Like, they were incredible.

I know that power is in me, but it's hard to see, to feel in groups of people. And I'm like, what's wrong with me?

My voice breaks into sobs.

Bonnie

No, no, it's a simple thing. All I want to do is take two wires from you and rewire them.

What I don't see you doing is contemplative awareness of yourself and loving yourself. And say I am the I am, that I am, I am.

That's the kind of meditation I want you to do. After you grieve this out, that's the mediation you should be doing. Energy goes out, so start within. Go into a deep contemplative awareness, Budha-style centered awareness.

When you condemn yourself for failure and for not hitting your mark, you're cutting off the connection that serves you. You're cutting them out.

So, as odd as this sounds, you want to switch your meditation soon, where you're going into insane internalization.

Elisa

I would love that. I'd absolutely love that.

Bonnie

We can see. We know you have all this power that you can feel. But can we stabilize it, like a zero-point field? Can we stabilize that and hold it? So that's why you're being asked to do more than the average man because we're asking you to stabilize a jet engine.

So, when you go into this meditative process, it's this part I'm speaking with, you're focusing on breath coming in and breath going out.

Then come back to your breath, then things will merge around you. Maybe psychic images or a longing for God. Come back to your breath.

And no astral traveling!

Bonnie (laughing)

I'm taking away your keys. I want you to stay put, centering, and stabilizing at zero point.

Start here; we'll get there. And I will tell you this, it's an interesting little tidbit, and you don't need me. But I find it fascinating that our paths have crossed, and I'm so driven to help you at any cost.

Bonnie(laughing)

And you probably see me as a nut case...

Bonnie(laughing again)

And you should. But Gaia and I think it's going well, and I think I'll be on there. And it is going great, but they're hung up on me because of the podcasts, the interviews. Of which you were one of three interviews. That's why I can see how things may evolve. This isn't to overstate my worth. It's the Universal algorithm that what will most likely pull you in front of an audience are the things you did by the seat of your pants, not because of all the hustling you've done to 'come, come, come to my retreats."

Does that make sense?

People will help you, Elisa. I don't know why that doesn't cross your mind.

You think you have to do this yourself because you're the Savior, and you are the Savior, God knows!

But I've worked my tail off and harassed many media producers and media people. Harassed them! So that we, so that people like you don't have to do all that work, so people like me can help you get there. And I love doing it.

My point is, I don't think it crosses your conscious awareness that there are people doing a lot of the hustle work, or the painful work, so that you can come in because you've already done that in another lifetime. We don't need you to do that. That's a waste of your time. We need you to just speak your truth and to procure and sustain and connect, have connections to a higher field of information, and then be able to hold that while someone puts a camera in your face, and speak fluently, without being afraid.

I'm really excited about where we're all going and you're going. You're going to get there.

It's funny. You think you're going to do this through your own forums. I see you doing more Ted Talk-type things, which the forums are begging for. I think you're going to get a lot more help and resources and people who want to help you from a whole different angle of humanity than you might expect. Sometimes I love being right. I love it when people record our calls.

I'm like, hmmm...we can go back, and I'll say I told you so.

We both laugh.

Chapter Ten

On 2/22/22, I had another session with Bonnie.

Bonnie

Survival in the energetic plane is not necessarily good or bad, and the hazing of 'survival' is meant for a very seasoned soul, or maybe the strongest among us, to go through those primal beginnings. Such as "I don't know if I'll have enough food or a house." We didn't fall. We didn't miss the happy boat because we had the default of survival. The way I see it from my perspective is that "elite souls start at ground zero," and it's gummy.

There is a plane of existence going on with you, in the root center, survival.

This is where you're stuck.

There is a life of you in the sacral.

There's a life of you in the solar plexus, quite powerful.

Bonnie(laughing)

There's a life of you in the heart center, quite powerful, all the crowds, all the people.

There's a heart-centered third-eye life going on. I think you're probably levitating. And there's a crown chakra life where you're like, I am the I am that I am, you know, I'm the I Am, that I Am, or whatever.

So, the idea is to allow oxygen and energy to move, like kundalini, to move from the root to the crown, root to the crown.

What's been happening to you because, again, you're what we call "the chosen one" or connected to these higher illusions. As you are starting into this survival mentality, you can feel locked into those lower levels. The idea is to be able to feel fluid motion up and down. Sometimes, I hit a transcendental state: beautiful. I want to go down and feel survival. Beautiful, I want to go up and down, scanning these dimensions. You're kind of learning to access all these dimensions freely and easily, so the thing here is the unlocking of the movement. And it's kind of funny when you get the hang of this. Your life will be falling apart, but you'll be laughing. It's because you can access high and low at the same time, and that creates something called centrifugal force. And when you have centrifugal force, then we get into our little zero-point buddy, and we get into that magnetism thing that we talked about instead of going outside yourself. And it creates this trust in yourself, as you're conscious of the stages that you go through.

You need both states, high and low, to turn the wheel. That's what causes this magnetism to happen. It allows you to become in sync with nature.

Bonnie(after a pause)

But here's the pitfall...getting stuck in the mind again.

You're going to have to be able to catch that when you need another cabin visit, or you need five minutes, or you need another shower. You hit a transcendental state in that shower in Utah, but you may not today.

I want you to have a claircognizant, somatic knowing that you are in union with higher planes, or you're not, and you know it.

That's the model, the radical new protocol, getting yourself to the spherical shape of coherence, where there's a trust of everything. Moving out from the ladder movement into the spherical shape of coherence. You don't like it, but you realize it's a part of everything.

Our guides are always talking. Sometimes, we hear it from our root chakra, and sometimes, we hear it from our third eye.

Part of what happens in this spherical experience is there is trust in everything. Even when it's hitting the fan, you trust.

You're strengthening your container. These interactions cultivate the container to hold a higher realm. It's not that they're not coming to you.

Can you hold it? Can you get in touch with the truth of who you've been? When you talk about this being that's held the cycle of eternity and light, your stomach turns to me, your energy goes cocky wobble because you touch it, and there's something so primal in you that becomes heartbroken. I can't explain it to you. You're so excited, and something in you is longing for it. It's so deep. It's the only time you quiver on the call.

Or your purpose, you quiver. Not a bad thing, not a good thing. It's the intensity of who you are when you touch it. It's learning to stabilize itself. You're always interpreting the information your guides are giving you. It's just from different planes of consciousness. All are relevant, and all are good.

Elisa

Do you see fear there when I talk about other people I've been?

Bonnie

It's not fear. It's an energy break, like a break line.

Elisa

It's trust. I don't fully trust it. It feels so *big*, and yet I have nothing. It's exhausting and overwhelming all at the same time.

Bonnie

Then, that's where you start. Getting back to the *I Am That I Am* and learning to trust in the reality of who you are.

Here's the process. This is real life. It's fear, its fear struck. And then my biology feels sick, and my tummy feels tight, and I'm closed. I'm out of coherence.

Then my mind is like, what if I never get back?

The way to get back is by identifying non-ordinary events.

Your life, your guides, speak to you from two different planes. They speak to you through your shower meditations, through feeling, through your sensory and psychic systems, through meditations, etc.

They also speak externally through synchronicities.

Everything is born from patterns. Everything is a pattern. When there is an anomaly, it's how your life can shake you awake and help you receive a new piece of information.

Transcendental moments can happen every single day. If you can, tune into them.

And when this happens, you're in your donut, in coherence. And you're co-creating.

That's the practice, and it will change your life.

Chapter Eleven

U ncertain the outcome but more uncertain I couldn't continue to live and exist the way I was, I did my homework. I purposely spent time intentionally strengthening my confidence and faith in myself.

I was encouraged by Bonnie to read a book titled *Dancing in the Shadows of the Moon*, where the author discusses the multidimensional nature of our souls and our true purpose when we come to Earth; to remember the truth of who we are.

From the information I gathered in this book and additional knowledge I channeled in my showers, I felt compelled and pulled to discover and learn 12 of my lifetimes, as I felt their experiences were important for the work, I was to do in this one. The images of description and explanation appeared much like a cartoon in my mind's eye. I saw our OverSouls (OS) fractalize into individual soul-rays (ISRs), came to understand realities and dimensions, and was shown the importance of what I call the *Twelve Perspectives* or also called the *144*.

The 12 channeled ISR lives appeared in my mind's eye much like faces on a clock; each ISR helping to energetically balance and harmonize the whole to gain the '144 perspective' necessary for spiritual advancement.

Was this the "Team of 12" Lisa had been talking about?

This perspective also explained the reason and necessity for there being 12 different but similar Earth realities, each with its own Jesus, Beyonce, or Donald Trump. As it allows for God to have the full experience as well. Following a shower meditation, I wrote this direct quote in my journal: "There are 12 different souls who play the same role in 12 different sister realities. In essence, there are 12 different perspectives of the same individual life.

A good example of this is the Spiderman movie, *No Way Home* where they talk about this fact and explain how there are three Peter Parkers.

On the Earth plane, we're comprised of our physical bodies and our ISR for that specific lifetime. Each ISR or life is connected to its Oversoul (or what I would envision as my higher self), an evolutionary Being of lifetimes, experiences, and wisdom not living within the constraints of time or space. Every lifetime and experience our Oversoul has occurs simultaneously as a refracted self.

Each refraction, or ISR, is unique, given its own unique life experiences and specific spiritual qualities, necessary for evolutionary growth.

In addition, each and every Oversoul has a direct, energetic connection to God, for His own experience, and as a connection to a direct healing source.

Also known as the Zero Point Field.

Every very Oversoul has countless refractions, living, operating, and experiencing all at the same time. Each available for us to tap into and receive insight, learning, understanding, and awareness. When we "tap in," we connect to our higher selves, our guides, and God, a practice we can cultivate during meditation.

The life of an individual soul ray (ISR) operates far beyond the Earth's normal death/life cycle and includes a pre-existence, a physical lifetime experience, and an afterlife experience.

When we incarnate in physical form, we have the ability to connect and access all other dimensions within our reality. Whether the angelic realm, another lifetime, or loved ones in the afterlife, though we may not be aware or conscious, this is possible or occurring. One such example is when we've had a loved one who's passed, and they come for a visit. Maybe dropping a coin or feather where we find it. Other times, we actually see or feel them, if only briefly.

My family has experienced this.

My sister Windy has visited multiple times. Walking into a room and suddenly smelling what her house smelled like, the time she told me to go outside and 'let go" by stirring up the trees and being "windy," visiting Emi in the shower and rubbing her face, or coming to Taylor moments before stepping on stage, holding her and whispering, "You've got this."

This is accessing other dimensions. Both Windy, in accessing ours, as well as us accessing hers.

The same is true in accessing multiple past lives to both learn and heal from.

Our job, through evolution, is to consciously become aware of this fact while learning to actively access all dimensions available to our refracted soul, letting us operate with a greater, more conscious, and expanded sense of the self.

When I channeled this, I already knew several of my lives but did not know all twelve. I was currently aware of myself, Jesus, Joan of Arc, Princess Diana, an Egyptian princess, the illegitimate daughter of Queen Elizabeth the 1st, and a 300-year-old monk. One day, in my shower and meditative space, I asked to be shown my other lives. I suddenly began seeing several flashing images and then saw myself as a spiritual Chinese warrior and defender of truth and good. He lived during a time of Chinese repression and fought hard for justice to prevail. In my flash of images, I watched as he was pierced by a sword through the chest while on his back, trying to crawl away.

I was then taken to a fairy forest where I saw myself as a fairy warrior, one involved in defending the Earth's realm against dark forces wanting to take control. In it, I watched myself die in battle.

Immediately upon my death, I saw myself as a Tibetan monk in a monastery high up in the mountains. I even watched myself levitate. I also felt his goodness and kindness.

Several days later, in another shower meditation, I saw and understood more of Jesus' time in the Garden of Gethsemane. His knowledge of manifesting and working with energy was incredibly skilled, allowing him to manifest what he needed whenever it was needed. And he never went without, working closely with nature sprites for nourishment, sustenance, and to sustain his body energetically and physically.

I also saw and felt my purpose and destiny is to fulfill and tap into the same abilities that Jesus had...learning to operate fully within a multidimensional world and eventually reaching the process of ascension, as he himself did.

And as many other Masters throughout the centuries on Earth have done.

However, the difference for me is that he had all the tools and skills taught to him from a young age and he brought in less generational trauma than most of us, as he was conceived via light conception. He also didn't have to "remember" being taught how to be in that space from the time he was born.

My job is to tap in, climb my way out of this "fall from grace," and use the same tools Jesus used and mastered, thereby showing others it's possible to get out from under the negative energy patterns, step into the fullness of who I am, and start mastering the same laws he did. Going right along with my life path number of eight.

Direct journal quote from 4/20/22 following that shower meditation. "My spiritual purpose is to attain full ascension as JC did, starting with very little conscious knowledge regarding my truth and inundated with the generational crap we're all born into, to knowing and purposely choosing interdimensional. Expanding on my gifts and developing an absolute "knowing" of energy and alchemy. Manifesting something out of thin air to walking on water."

Several days later, I was in Utah with Taylor and Bella for a dance competition where they were both competing in their solos. Bella and I were at the convention center while she was warming up, and she did not appear happy. She had a scowl on her face, her eyes were downcast, and she didn't appear particularly motivated. I started looking around the convention center and noted a similar attitude with the majority of other kids and their parents. It felt tense everywhere.

Suddenly, I had the thought, "I needed to clear the convention center space." Not knowing if it would help, I closed my eyes, grounded myself, and stated, "I command that this space be filled with pure, divine light and energies only. Any and all energies wanting to negatively influence are to be removed *immediately!*" Then, I said with greater force, "It is *done*, it is *done*, it is *done*!!!"

While making the statement, I visualized light coming through and pushing out, clearing the space.

"Michael, I ask that you please take the *negative energies* and dispose of them where they can't affect us anymore. Thank you.

Upon opening my eyes, the entire convention center felt brighter, lighter, and better. I glanced at Bella, her face shinier, and she was gaping at me.

"What did you do?" she asked.

"You felt that?" I replied.

"Yes," she said.

"Wow, I just cleared the space," I said, smiling. "Hopefully, it helps."

And help it did. I noticed her entire attitude changed, and so did the rest of the building. I immediately sent the intention to Michael and others to set up an energy grid of protection for the rest of the weekend.

This clearing was an incredible confirmation to me that we most definitely live in a multidimensional world with energies that do not want us to succeed. Not wanting us to feel joy, love, or peace. The high-frequency emotions that make us feel good.

Instead, they want us to feel low, sad, angry, and shameful so they can feed off of us, like psychic vampires.

Several days later, exactly the same as when it occurred with Jesus, the name Elizabeth Taylor popped into my head at the moment of my awakening. And in the same realization and way as before, I was hit with the "knowing" that I'd been her, and she me.

Was it really true? Elizabeth Taylor, as well? I'd heard of the possibility of having one concurrent life within the same reality. Was it possible to have several at a time? Already Diana and I'd been alive at the same time; I was born shortly before she was married, not much older than her boys. And in the case of Elizabeth Taylor, we were all three alive, at the same time, for almost 18 years.

The enormity of this information was huge and honestly hard to fathom. Some days, my faith and trust felt solid. On other days, the incessant thoughts of "I'm not enough" or "I'm crazy to think I could have been all those people" took my confidence and trust to near zero. I was nowhere close to finding balanced coherence.

Regardless, the synchronicities kept coming.

Somewhere during the summer of 2022, I started watching documentaries about Elizabeth. One of them talked about the first movie she made and showed pictures of her actor's chair and name where they'd spelled her name wrong. Instead of spelling it Elizabeth, it read _Elisabeth_ Taylor. The exact spelling of my first name within hers.

Is that why I've thought several times throughout my life that if I wanted, I could be an actor?

I've never acted outside of playing a snippet of Shakespeare's Juliet in a play put on by my church group when I was 12. Unless you count the time in my high school behavioural science class when I created a talk-show video pretending to be someone with multiple personalities, my inspiration coming from Sally Fields when she played the role of Cybil. The video appeared real enough, I found out the teacher was still playing it for his students over ten years later.

But I've never felt compelled, never tried out, never wondered about, and never wanted that path. And yet...the thought has come to me several times throughout my life, "I could be an actor if I wanted."

More interestingly, we named our oldest Taylor Ann.

Synchronicities.

In January of 2023, while in Costa Rica, I read my first book about Elizabeth Taylor titled, _Elizabeth Taylor, The Grit and Glamour of An Icon_ by Kate Andersen Brower. In it were several _ahas_ and other synchronicities. The author mentions Elizabeth's pain when she learns Diana is killed, saying, "I know what it's like to be chased in a car by the paparazzi, and it's one of the most frightening, claustrophobic feelings in the world. You're in a car, you're going faster and faster, trying to get away from them. They can shoot through darkened windows, and you end up in a corner of the car."

Were Elizabeth's fears and the horrific death experienced by Diana why between 6 – 8 years old, I had recurrent dreams of being in a car and going off a cliff? Waking moments before I hit the ground?

The dreams heavily influenced my trust in others and for a period of several years, I didn't want to ride with anyone other than my parents. Even now at the age of 44, my biggest fear comes as a passenger in a car, affecting me every time we drive. I typically find myself forcibly calming my nerves with deep breaths and often have to ask the driver to slow down around corners.

The fear was heightened when my teenage girls started to drive, forcing me to finally seek healing work with tuning forks and vibrational sound therapy. Though better managed it's still a fear I deal with every time I get in a car.

Diana's death was impactful enough Elizabeth felt inclined to release a press statement saying she thought the paparazzi had murdered Diana, though they'd briefly met only once before.

Even more interesting, a few weeks prior to Diana's death, Elizabeth was at the Ritz in Paris and had the same drunk driver Diana had. He'd been inclined to go fast then, too, to which Elizabeth responded, "No way."

Synchronicities.

They were both heavily impactful in the HIV community and helped change the perception with which it was viewed, that those with HIV can be held, loved, and touched. Something I feel very strongly about as well. In addition, we should be doing everything possible to protect those most vulnerable to catching it. And we should be doing everything possible to find a cure, which I believe the right frequency can do.

And in contrast to many religions, I've never felt my friends and family who are gay, transgender, or LGBTQ, are anything but perfect souls who've agreed to experience an avatar life as gay.

Many themselves are highly evolved souls with a specific goal to raise awareness, consciousness, and our Earth's frequency.

In truth, our souls are genderless, and we are attracted to others energetically, whether in ethereal or physical form. The attraction is less about the physical sex characteristics and more about the attraction and energy exchange that occurs between two people.

And though genderless, our souls often have a preference in how they appear to others, whether male or female.

Is this why so many feel they're in the wrong body? Because at their soul level, they prefer being in the *form* of the opposite sex?

I've thought multiple times about why so many individuals feel they're in the wrong body. It makes sense there would be those who, while their soul prefers being a certain sex; in this soul ray lifetime, they agreed and contracted to *experience* an avatar as the sex they don't prefer.

But for many, the soul yearns for what it desires and is enormous for some. As I've seen with many of my patients in the transgender community.

I believe, however, that where we've gone off track is to start hormone therapy or sexual realignment surgery for someone to transition when their brain isn't fully matured or developed, as they're still trying to figure out who they are and what they desire. Unfortunately, kids (and even adults) can be easily inundated with ideas and belief systems to believe it's something they want, whether by their peers, medical doctors, or their parents and family members.

Most of it is subconscious in nature.

I'd rather a kid wait for their transition surgery until they're at least 18 and after completing important counseling and educational classes. This will give them a better understanding of what transitioning will mean for them.

I believe the worst thing that can happen is having someone regret their irreversible decision simply because they didn't know it wasn't something they didn't really want.

The rest of my Twelve and how they are integrated with all that I have been discussing were discovered through a process similar to past life regressions, which I completed with a gifted healer in Australia. In those sessions, I remembered being a scientist in WW II, held against my will, whose work on frequency and the creation of disease were suppressed and kept from the public. In this particular regression, I saw myself create and destroy diabetes and cancer in the lab, with specific frequency changes.

Lastly, I saw myself as a little boy living a life of homelessness, fear, and in survival mode.

Experiencing the yin and yang.

I've been avatars in monogamous lifetimes, married or attached to one person. I've also been married and had multiple partners in other lives. I've experienced lack and financial struggle as well as having no financial constraints, traveling the world on yachts, with nannies, and having every need attended to. I've been cheated on and cheated on others; I've been the narcissist and the victim. I've also raised and inspired an army and walked on water. And yes, I've even played for the dark side (though I've since chosen which side I stay on), as the cultivation of our souls requires a full experience for evolutionary and spiritual growth. Many of these experiences the result of karmic energies, contractual agreements, and generational patterns.

My Twelve, as I call them, for this evolutionary cycle, give me access to the 144 perspective and understanding, helping me form the cohesive framework required for higher-level functioning, progress, and evolution in a multidimensional world. Every lifetime and perspective is necessary and valid, but obviously different, and brings with it necessary information for us to utilize in our current ISR life. Even though subconscious for most of us, throughout multiple lifetimes and/or for a huge part of each life. In some, we start to remember and begin to play inter-dimensionally. In others, we continue to play out the amnesia the 3D Earth experience brings us. But the patterns, learning, and karmic relationships all play out for each of us, all of the time.

When I channeled the evolutionary process it appeared like an animated video game, showing me a series of levels and mastery, one must attain to advance. Within each level, the Oversoul plays out 12 different lives: 12 different avatars, if you will. All balancing, harmonizing, supporting, and playing out karma, contracts, and what the Oversoul requires for advancement to the next spiritual level.

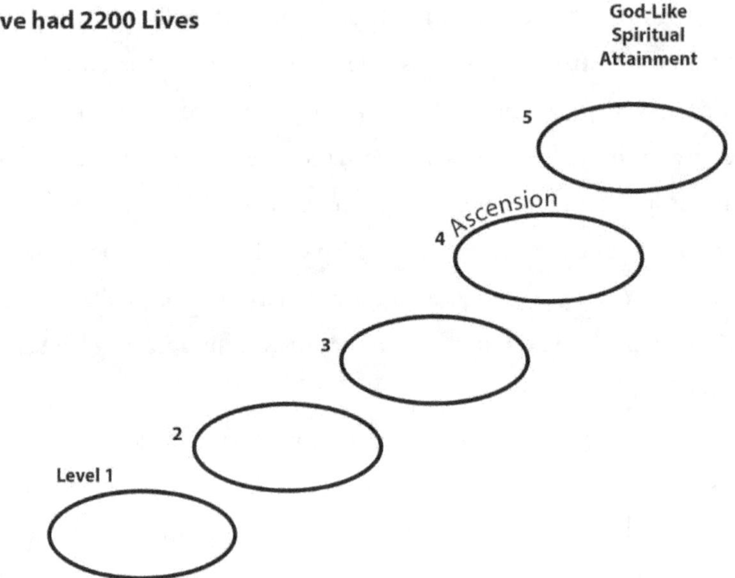

Each level consists of 12 ISRs, similar to numbers on a clock. I envision a group of 12 ISRs sitting in a room with other members of their soul family discussing, planning for, and agreeing to experiences they'll have in their upcoming ISR life. Each ISR agrees to experience certain events, a specific career, emotional trauma, or take on certain generational and spiritual gifts, negative or positive. Every ISR is energetically balancing the other by fulfilling karmic debts or paybacks and taking on specific life purposes, often consciously unknown to the ISR individual while here on Earth. And every dimension, or level, of 12 lives has an individualized purpose or experience being sought, with the ultimate goal of spiritual advancement.

One Level of Avatars/Lives

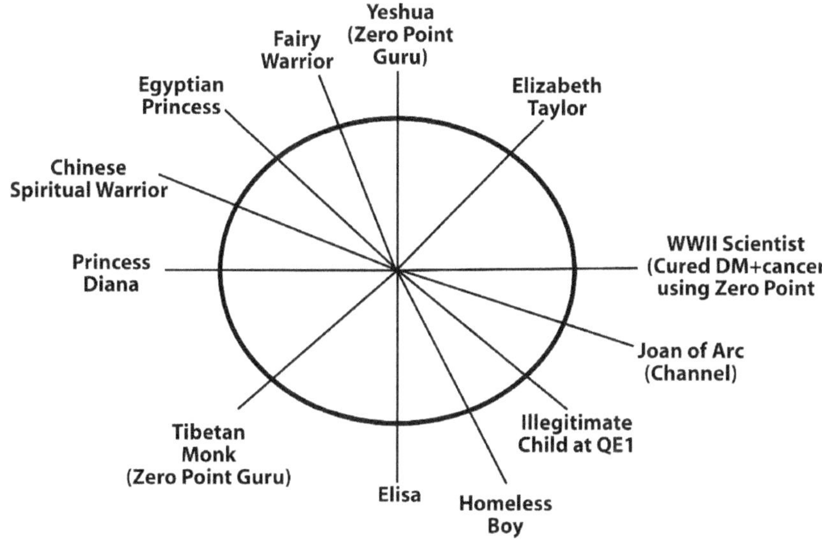

My purpose for this level is Ascension

In each lifetime, spiritual characteristics and gifts come from multiple sources. There are astrological, numerological, genetic, current lifetime and OverSoul influences. OverSoul characteristics are who we are at the core of our being and what we've been cultivated into through eons of experiences. Not all spiritual gifts the OverSoul carries come through in each lifetime, though through experience and growth, we can learn to tap into these gifts inter-dimensionally.

Please note when I say advancement, one typically thinks better. It is not better. It just is. It's where the particular soul is at any given time, and we're all souls at different levels of understanding, growth, and awareness. It's not good or bad.

It just is.

A classic example is my daughter Emi, as this is her first life as a human, meaning she's a fairly new soul. As far as we know, she's been a horse, a butterfly, and a dog, but never human. Something we've heard from multiple psychics at different times throughout Emi's life. None of them knowing each other.

By contrast, Taylor and Bella have been hundreds upon hundreds of different avatars.

In fact, I believe that Bella was or is Queen Elizabeth the First, and I was one of her illegitimate children in that life. And I believe that my husband Brian was Michael Todd during my life as Elizabeth.

I also know Taylor, Windy, and I were together during my life as an Egyptian Princess and I believe my Mom was my mother Mary during my life as Jesus, as was shown to me in a past life regression.

Chapter Twelve

As noted earlier, I began looking for work in January, particularly for what I was willing to do. I began speaking with companies and searching locally for anything available. In February, I was contacted by a friend from Bend who had just opened her own medical aesthetics office, and she was looking for a medical director.

It wasn't a full-time job but would require me to go to Bend, OR, once a month and spend two to three days. While there, I'd have the opportunity to see patients and clients in the area.

I said yes.

One job down, another to go.

At some point in April, I began speaking with a local company looking for a doctor to cover the local prison in Kuna, ID. It consisted of 12-hour shifts, two days a week, lasting two to three months. It seemed the perfect interim job, though I struggled with what I considered as "going back into the traditional medical system," a restrictive system missing key components for efficiency and overall health. Nevertheless, we needed the money, and this would help provide it. The job was set to begin at the end of May after weeks of paperwork, credentialing, and onboarding.

A couple weeks before training began, the recruiter reached out for clarification on the answer I put asking about cannabis usage. I responded that yes, I use it and, in fact, fully support it. I then sent her a link to an episode in my Quantal U series about the incredible healing benefits of cannabis and my story for why I use it.

Two weeks later, I was scheduled for a drug test, and while the results were pending, I began the onboarding process. I was scheduled to start work the very next day. But the next morning, the recruiter called and said there was cannabis in my system.

"Yes, I was open about that with you," I said.

"I'm sorry," she said. "But it's not allowed."

I was shocked; I had just spent two months getting paperwork filled out, going through the credentialing process, and being completely honest about my cannabis use. Suddenly, I couldn't work for them.

In addition, I'd spent eight hours training the day before, to which she said she couldn't pay me.

What the fuck.

Trying to salvage what I could, I quickly wrote a letter explaining my experience. I work in Oregon, and have for several years, where it's legal. During that time, I've had the opportunity to see the benefits of cannabis up close and personal. Many of my patients were alcohol or drug addicts and even heavily medicated veterans, coming to me on their trifecta of addictive drugs: benzos, narcotics, and sleeping pills.

Most of them wanted similar scripts or increased dosages as their years of use rendered the medication less efficacious. But, I was not a fan of these medications. Over the years, I'd seen addiction after addiction and much of my training was spent learning about and doing our best to limit and/or reduce the number of people affected. And it was a lot.

The massive healthcare costs for addicts alone were insane, totaling more than 3.73 trillion dollars annually.

I saw them often, sometimes several times each day, whether doctor shopping, at the weekend urgent care clinic, or through the ED. The intensity and number of people seeking controlled substances and medications were drastically increasing, along with my patience and willingness to prescribe. Thankfully, cannabis was legalized in 2016 and I took a front-row seat in watching it evolve, encouraging many of my patients to use a high CBD/THC combination oil for overall pain, sleep, and inflammation.

Over the next few years, I watched it help various conditions. Rashes, autoimmune diseases, chronic pain, depression, cancer remissions, and more. Story after story after story of improvement and healing. Not everyone, but more than 70% of people responded positively. Many of them getting rid of their more addictive medications.

Dealing with my own pain, folded lateral meniscus in the middle of my knee, and chronic neck and shoulder pain, cannabis was the only thing I would take. After my experience with ketoprofen, I never wanted to use narcotics again, knowing my propensity for addiction.

And, with the profound impact cannabis had on my mood, sleeping patterns, and pain, I didn't want to try anything else.

Regardless, the letter didn't matter. Though my recruiter understood and agreed with my position, her hands were tied.

They weren't budging. I'd lost the job.

Devastated, I fell into an emotional vortex of pain, anger, frustration, and shame. The emotions were low enough that I stayed in them for the entirety of the month of June. Everything was difficult. Every thought was negative, and every interaction was painful. I was pummeled with negative thoughts throughout the day, thoughts I began thinking and saying about myself.

I felt emotionally blunted, had difficulty expressing happiness when others were around, and felt hard and angry. And the thoughts were incessant. I found myself isolating, keeping to myself, and not wanting to socialize or hang out.

I began having thoughts of not wanting to be here and wishing I was done. It was too hard, and I was all alone.

And I had failed...yet again, and with it, the guarantee for consistent income was gone.

I wasn't afraid of death. I knew what existed beyond the 3D Earth. Anything had to be better than here.

But no matter how hopeless it seemed or how worthless I felt, I could not leave my family behind.

There was no way I'd leave them to clean up and deal with the aftermath, dealing with their own trauma of a mother who ended her life because she couldn't deal. Couldn't seem to make it happen. She couldn't grow her business like she promised, bringing in a similar salary to the one she used to have. I would be leaving my husband to entirely raise our three girls. Also, he would receive no financial compensation for my death, as I had no life insurance at that time.

That would've been the shittiest thing to do to those I loved. I couldn't, and I wouldn't. I loved them too much.

At the end of June, several days before returning to Souls With Stamina as a small group leader, the 8-day retreat I've attended every summer, I was in Bend, OR, for my medical director job. I still felt super low, but I continued the job search throughout the month. I was tired of having *no* money in our account much of the time, staying home, and not being social simply because I couldn't afford even a coffee among friends. I was also becoming resentful and angry. Everything in life sucked, no matter how hard I worked, how positive I acted, or how much I manifested, through gratitude, what I wanted; life kept giving me shit.

I felt done and was having a hard time believing any of the things I had been told about myself in the last two years were either real or possible.

Was it all a joke? I really was crazy. Thinking I had a big purpose I was supposed to do.

The thoughts kept coming and coming.

Thankfully, I had another job set to start in August, working for a body sculpting medical aesthetics company. I had been in contact with them since early May and had interviewed with them. I was now waiting to schedule a time for training in Idaho Falls at one of their other facilities. I was excited as it was procedural in nature, something I'd missed since leaving traditional medicine. And it was outside insurance mandates, policies, and meaningful use measures, as the procedures are elective and for aesthetic purposes only.

It seemed the perfect job with which to guarantee a sizeable, consistent income each week.

This week, I was in Bend, at the home of the spa owner, Elena, where I'd stay whenever I came into town. While there, I was asked to see the son of one of her good friends, whom I'll call James. He'd recently lost a ton of weight and started meditating in the last several weeks. However, he had recently begun acting strangely, seeing things and talking to people others couldn't see.

As soon as I saw him, I knew James was interdimensional. He was speaking with his guides, astral traveling, and seeing the Universe in a way he'd never seen before. He was also having a hard time understanding it, and so was his family, who were rightfully scared. I did my best to help him ground and understand what was happening. I consciously ran energy, visualizing the stabilization process so he could better deal with all he was seeing and feeling. After an hour, he seemed much better, and I left for home, promising to return the next day.

When I returned to his house, James was sitting on an outside swing, and I sat with him. He seemed more tranquil and relaxed but still very anxious and uncertain. Some in his family wanted to take him to the hospital, and I was hoping to help him understand and be consciously aware of what was happening. Hoping to keep him stable.

At one point in our conversation, he looked at me and said, "When you were working on me yesterday, I could see that you were drawing from dark and light, and I was really confused."

I looked up shocked, suddenly feeling embarrassed and completely vulnerable. Here I was, the doctor, and educating him on what he was experiencing, and he said this? What was he talking about? I would never consciously draw from the dark, never.

"It's an energy you drew in because you're being hateful to someone. You're talking mean about someone," James said.

And in that instance, that moment, I knew.

"The only person I speak unkindly towards is myself," I said, bringing immediate tears to my eyes.

"Yes, that's it," he replied.

After leaving his house, I sobbed. I had been incredibly mean to myself, beyond. Most thought processes throughout the day were hateful and putting myself down in some way. I knew how the game worked. I was fully aware of what my thoughts could and could do. And yet, I succumbed. I allowed them to overtake my psyche and allowed the negative energy of those thought processes to enter my field. So, even when I was helping others with good intentions, I was also drawing on this negative energy.

I was set to arrive at SWS the next day and was in no emotional state to assist anyone else there. I couldn't help with healing and raising one's frequencies when pulling from such a low place of shame and guilt.

When I woke the next morning, I knew I'd find comfort in my trees. Since April 2020, I've developed a special relationship with the trees, often using them as places of solace and seeking answers. The "forest" close to our house then had a tree I called "Mother," a large, dead tree you see as you first enter the woods. Most of it had fallen, but the base stood erect and strong, bits of it falling or blowing away day by day. My first experience with her was powerful. I had taken mushrooms for the first time and was in the forest on a hike. As soon as I saw her, I watched her breath (a frequent and wonderful side effect of the mushrooms), and then I touched and could feel her movement, her return embrace. The emotion was so intense I cried with happiness and feelings of love. From that moment on, she was there whenever I needed a release. I could put my arms around her and let go.

Time after time, I'd visit her, releasing the moment we'd touch, the tears easily flowing. When we moved to Florida, I'd find the biggest banyan tree I could find to sit next to and be with. When we moved to Boise, I created my sanctuary in the shower. I waited to connect with the trees when we'd go into the mountains, something I'd do approximately once a month.

Today, the trees were calling my name. I felt the pull bigger than anything, so I decided to stop on my way from Bend to Salem. The drive there is spectacular in and of itself, winding its way through Sisters, OR, and the beauty of the Mackenzie River. Many of the trees are giant pine and ponderosas, leaving behind a beautiful auburn ground and giving incredible protection to animals and humans alike. They're both majestic and sacred, and that's where I wanted to go.

Finding an easy turn-off, I drove about five minutes in, parked the car, and stepped out, seeing an alcove of trees right in front of me.

As soon as I stepped into the alcove, I started sobbing. Large, fat, crocodile tears spilled down my cheeks, splattering the ground and landing on ants as they crawled by. After a while, I started saying I was sorry to myself over and over. "I'm so sorry. I love you. I'm so sorry I said all those things. I'm so sorry I thought all those things. I'm so sorry. Please forgive me," I said over and over.

For over half an hour, I cried, releasing, apologizing, and forgiving myself. Eventually, the crying ebbed and came to a stop. I was exhausted but felt lighter than I had in months.

I got back in my car and drove the rest of the way to Salem. SWS was exactly what I needed, and the intense respite before arriving seemed to do the trick. I felt alive, vibrant, and glad to be there, along with the rest of my family. In addition, I had an amazing small group of individuals to oversee for the week. My mom and I were on the medical team for the week, giving me multiple opportunities to practice my gifts and skills.

I was a conduit and ran a source of energy, augmenting healing for people in pain or injured. I watched as my medicine cabinet of essential oils soothed headaches and rashes and helped decrease swelling. In addition, I worked with Archangel Michael to remove entities and spirits from both the person and the property, there to wreak havoc on the week.

And havoc they did.

Until we cleared them.

I held sessions helping others clear limiting beliefs and generational patterns not serving them.

All in all, the week was everything "woo-woo," and I was exactly where my heart always wanted to be.

One of the most powerful energy clearings I have ever done for myself was during this week of SWS. While the forest release several days earlier was essential and necessary, I still had a lot of anger, shame, and sadness about the last couple of years.

Because no matter how you look at it...I was a failure.

Everything I had set out to do, accomplish, teach, educate, and reach people about had failed. I'd spent tens upon tens of thousands of dollars on my website, branding, marketing, and creating. But regardless, and time after time, I could not reach enough people to start building a solid, stable business.

And part of the incessant thoughts I'd been having the past month had centered around this.

I was angry, and I felt isolated and alone.

On top of that, I knew intuitively that COVID was not what MSM pretended it to be, and I felt the ultimate intent was for depopulation and mass control. On a grander and multidimensional scale, this was a spiritual war between good and evil.

And it often felt like we were losing.

I was sickened by the astronomical number of COVID vaccination injuries and angry at my colleagues for blindly going against reason and logic.

I felt terribly for those suffering from long-term issues related to the virus, the vaccine, mass psychosis, censorship, and the division created in the last couple of years.

I did not want to hold these low-frequency emotions any longer, as their effects were debilitating. More than anything, I knew I needed to start the process of clearing them, and I knew just the one.

Sand, Tree, Rock.

In this energetic healing process, the person moves between each station, authentically bringing up the emotions they're feeling at each one, releasing them. Standing close by are two people helping you get into that feeling, saying things to trigger your emotional response.

By shaking the tree branch, we bring up and shake away our fears, releasing them to Mother Earth. The sand symbolizes the release of sadness and pain and letting it go, and the rock for beating the anger out.

The first time I ever saw the process was when I took Alchemy. At the time, I agreed to proxy for my Dad, helping him break up and release some of the emotional pain he'd suffered, as well as helping his generational line. At first, I was getting into the process and entering a zone. But as soon as I started, the upstairs door to the garage opened, and my dad walked into the house. The sound immediately snapped me out of it, and I couldn't fully get back.

To do the process and do it well, one had to be all in. They had to give it all they had and be as vulnerable as possible. That's where I saw the most benefit for the biggest shifts to occur. But it was hard, especially in such a big room, with everyone watching.

I saw it again in 2020 at SWS and watched as one of the biggest guys I know gave it his all. It was one of the most powerful experiences I'd ever witnessed. I knew one day I'd have my chance.

Chapter Thirteen

Weeks before arriving at SWS, I felt it was my year to finally complete sand, rock, and tree, and Lynell gave the OK. The day of, I could feel the energy building hours before the process. When it was my turn, I picked my two standing supporters, Cha and Pam, two people I knew would have my back.

I walked to the center and immediately went to the rock. The intensity continued to build, and even now, while writing this, I can feel it again. With the first hit of the rock onto the hardwood, I was in it.

I'm so angry!!!!!! I yelled, smack, smack, smack. I hit the wood as hard as possible. *WTF!!!* I'm all alone! Smack, smack, smack. No one to help! Smack, smack. The sound of each hit resounding through the room. In every life and lifetime, I'm all *alone!!!!* I screamed.

Aghhhhhhhhhhh!!!! I screamed, feeling a deep guttural roar rising from within me while continuing to hit the wood as hard as possible, each hit creating dents.

Aghhh!!! Smack

Aghhhh!!! Smack

Aghhh!!! Smack.

Over and over, I went. Finally, the strength began to leave my body as my muscles neared fatigue, and I sat firmly on my hunches for several seconds.

"Shall we move to sand or tree?" Char asked.

"No tree, I need sand," I replied, slowly rising and crawling my way to the sandbox.

Once I arrived, I started to sob.

"Please take the pain," I said.

"It's too much. I don't want it anymore. It isn't helping me. Please take my pain. Take the sadness, take the guilt, take the shame." I kept saying over and over.

"Please take the pain of the world, the cruelty of so many," I sobbed. "It's too much, too much."

"So many are suffering, now more than ever. Please, God, please take it."

"Release, release, release."

And then I felt the anger rise again in my body, and I turned back to the rock.

"Anger!" I yelled.

Smack, smack, smack.

"*I'm so fucking angry!!!!!*" I was screaming with such intensity that I thought it would tear out of me.

Smack! Smack!

"It's *too* much*!!*"

Smack!

"No *more!!!*"

Smack, smack, smack.

I continued, with similar verbiage, for an unknown amount of time until suddenly, I knew I was done.

I let the rock go and fell back, Lynell catching me in her arms.

"I love you, sweet Elisa," she said, whispering in my ear as she held me from behind. "That was beautiful."

Breathing hard, I slowly focused my eyes on the room around me. There, I saw Brian, Taylor, Bella, my niece and nephew Brooklan and Koen, and Taylor's boyfriend Lee looking at me with mixed expressions of concern, admiration, and love. Slowly, one by one, they came forward and hugged me.

I'd done it, fully let go, and wailed.

What an incredible feeling.

The other remarkable moment came at the end of the week when Lisa and I would once again sit down for a read.

I wanted to know if she saw anything more regarding my business, as I was losing hope Bodhi would ever become anything. I already lacked patience, a skill I'm working really hard at, and constantly asked God, "When already?!"

Lisa and I swapped in trade, and I was desperately seeking guidance.

"What should I be doing? How can I manifest more money? What is my next step?"

And I wanted to verify with her what I had learned regarding my past lives. One of her specialties is being able to see the past lives of those she reads and being a psychic.

Two years prior at SWS, in June of 2020, Lisa had mentioned to me, in passing, that she saw a business partner who'd be coming into my life.

I'd completely forgotten this information until I channeled a male business partner in early April 2021.

When I returned to SWS in July 2021, Lisa confirmed it again. I was on a 15-minute break and headed to my trailer to grab something I'd left there. Lisa was sitting at the picnic table in front of the Institute. As I walked by, she said, "I keep seeing a business partner of yours."

I immediately stopped, turned, and exclaimed, "You do?! Do you have a name?"

"Umm, it starts with a J, something like John, John?"

I gasped. I couldn't believe it. She'd just told me the nickname of the person I'd already channeled as working with me in the future.

The name of someone who'd been dead for several years already.

My body lit up with excitement.

"Wow!" What did this mean?

Did he really *not* die in that plane crash? Or did he die and this person is a twin-flame of him, as I am of Diana, Elizabeth, and others?

Or is it that he'll simply be aiding me from the spirit world side? Aiding me multidimensionally, Like Windy does.

It really got me thinking.

In 2020, she also told my Mom that she believed Elizabeth Taylor was one of my past lives, something she brought up when I told her I believed I'd been her.

And as already mentioned, she gave me a full read a year prior, verifying my past life with Diana.

That year, we sat in my trailer, sharing a bowl between us.

And as I was about to ask questions, Lisa began telling me what she was seeing.

She'd been helping with a not-for-profit with the goal to create re-entry and rehabilitative programs for alcoholics and drug addicts coming out of recovery. She was a prior addict, knowing the severe fallacies and flaws in the system, and she knew the recovery rate, at less than 10%, was not acceptable.

The programs would give individuals a safe space to continue in their recovery. Most importantly, the implemented programs would offer emotional, traumatic, generational, and integrative recovery work to further assist and guarantee someone a full recovery. The integrative therapies would include RET, sound healing, Reiki, mind-body medicine, and others, to name a few. In addition, they'd receive education on important life skills and understandings.

In the past year, the company had been working to raise money for the program and were looking for where to put the first center. Their considerations were someplace back East or in Idaho. She felt Idaho would be a great place and was thinking I might be their medical director.

"That would be my ideal job." I thought to myself. "What a God-send that would be."

However, I didn't put much further thought into it as the not-for-profit was in its early stages, and they still had to decide where to put the initial center. I knew that would be a while, and it wasn't something I could count on happening.

"We'll see how it pans out," I thought, and then said out loud, "I'm hoping you can verify lives I've channeled of myself, make sure I'm not crazy."

I laughed somewhat nervously.

She closed her eyes. "I'm seeing Brian, wait, wait. Does Brian sleep on this side of the bed?"

"Yes," I responded.

She laughed. "All I'm seeing is him."

"Ok, hold on, let me touch you," she said, placing a hand on my foot.

We sat quietly for several moments.

"Ok," she said. "Who would you like to know about?"

"Was I Joan of Arc?"

She paused. "Yes."

"Was I an Egyptian princess?"

"Umm, yes. I can see the big headdress you wore."

"Was I Elizabeth Taylor?"

"Yes, I told your Mom that before. Did you know that?!" she exclaimed.

"No, I didn't," I replied. "When was this?"

"The first summer you came to SWS for the week, the first time I saw your business partner. I didn't know you that well, but I told your Mom."

"That's cool," I said.

"Princess Diana?"

"Yes."

"A fairy."

"Umm...yes." She laughed. "A badass."

"A warrior," I said.

She made eye contact and replied, "Yes."

"A Chinese warrior."

"Oh, yes, definitely. You've had a lot of lifetimes in China."

"Interesting," I responded.

"Okay, how about Marilyn Monroe?"

"Umm, no, I'm sorry. Not her."

"Ok, how about Julia Roberts?"

"No," she laughed.

"How about a WWII German Scientist?"

"Yes, I see that. But not German," she said.

"Ok, interesting," I thought to myself. When I'd seen the images during my regressions with Ethereal Wings, I'd had the impression I was a scientist in WWII, forced to do his work, working for the Germans. I assumed this meant I was German, but maybe not. I'd have to meditate and ponder on this.

"The illegitimate child of Queen Elizabeth 1?" I asked.

"Yes," she said.

"Do you still think Bella was QE1?"

"Yes!" She exclaimed. "Most definitely."

"Was I Francis Bacon?" I asked. I'd had a lot of incoming synchronicities about him as of late. While not convinced I'd been him, I very much feel we worked in concert together. With everything he did, both in secret and in public.

"No," she replied.

Ok, I was finally ready, she'd been very confirming. I'd also thrown random names into the mix to see how she'd respond.

"Was I Christ?" I asked, my voice more hushed than before.

"You were..." She stopped mid-sentence.

"Hmm, interesting. I think you were!" she said, looking at me. "I keep seeing him with the male symbol and the female symbol."

"Like the divine masculine and the divine feminine," I thought to myself, remembering that Anna, Grandmother to Jesus, said something similar in her book.

"On page 110," she states. "I became aware that not only would my grandson represent the Father Godhead, but with that, his twin soul would also incarnate, joining with Mary Anna to bring down into the earth plane the full return of the Mother Godhead."

Twin-soul being analogous with twin-flame; meaning from the same OverSoul or better said fractals of the same soul consciousness. And as I'd seen during a past life regression, my mom in this life, was my mom in Jesus's, she being Mary Anna.

Confirmations.

"On page 138, Anna mentions Yeshua receiving the ceremonial necklace of Hathor at this birth, representing the union of male and female principles."

More confirmation.

"Wow, yes, the male and female symbols are both attached to him," Lisa said. "That indicates male and female."

I sat there in wonderment and awe.

"Thank you, Universe," I thought to myself. "Thank you for the confirmation."

At that moment, Taylor, Koen, and others arrived at the trailer for their reads.

We looked at each other, the moment quickly passing as she turned her focus to them.

When we left the Institute the next day, I felt renewed and excited for what was to come.

One week later, I arrived in Idaho Falls for my first two days of training. The staff was pleasant, and the clinic was adorable.

The work required good body posture and strength, as you're standing over a table, holding a vibrating tool for most of the day, something I wasn't used to, nor had done in quite a while.

Though slow, I enjoyed the work and knew my skills and confidence would grow. When I left, it was agreed I'd return for another two days of training in August. The clinic opening in Boise had been pushed back a month, and it was now looking to be at the beginning of September. I was beyond excited to finally bring consistent income into our bank accounts again.

A week later, Brian, Bella, Emi, and I left for a week-long trip down the middle fork of the salmon. It's a 100-mile stretch of river out in the middle of nowhere in Idaho, where the only way to experience it is to pull a permit *or* hire a company with rights to take you down. To say it's a trip of a lifetime would be an understatement.

The trip offered incredible scenery, animals, waterfalls, hot springs, sunsets, thrilling water, and so much more.

The last time I'd been down the middle fork was July of 2004 when Taylor was nine months old, and we were set to move to Missouri, starting medical school in August. Though Brian and I have been on many trips to many places since that time, it remains one of the best trips we've had together.

On the other hand, Brian had been down the middle fork numerous times. He went two to three times as a kid growing up and became a middle-fork rafting guide between semesters at college. After moving to medical school, he went another three times. Once with my family when my sister Becky pulled the permit in 2012, with his family in 2015, then again with his Dad in 2020. I, unfortunately, was in residency or working. Still, when my brother Rob called to ask if we were available, it was too good an opportunity to pass up, a true wish come true.

The trip was everything and more when we pulled off the river on August 7th. When we finally came into cell phone service, I started seeing the slew of text messages spilling into my phone, one from our landlord.

"The owners are not renewing, so I'm serving a 30-day notice today. They are moving to town and moving into it themselves. They will be scheduling an inspection to check the condition early next week."

The text was sent on August 1st; we were already a week in, and the girls were set to start school on August 15th.

"Here we go again," I thought.

During my shower mediation on Sunday morning, I listed our specifications and the total amount we'd be willing to spend. When I got out of the shower, I wrote our specifications down on paper.

"Ok, God," I thought. "This is what my family needs."

Though our house was okay at the time, it was far from ideal. My husband currently had his office out of the garage. Which worked most of the time unless we were taking the car in and out. On the other hand, I had put my office in the "open" dining room, attached to the living room. I was using a divider. However, it wasn't private and didn't allow me to have appointments when people were around.

What we needed were better options without the increase in our price point.

Taylor sent me several listings, and I found several others, narrowing our search down to two.

Amazingly, the two houses offered everything we needed, though, in one, Brian's office would still be in the garage. But, it was tucked away in a niche that would have provided a great space. And both were the same price. I couldn't believe our luck.

We said yes to the one which made the most sense and started packing. It was the easiest move we've ever had. Each person took apart and cleaned their own room, packed everything into boxes, and moved them into the trailer. By Saturday, we were packed and moved. On Sunday, I had my kitchen unpacked and my bedroom set up.

Just in time for school.

Chapter Fourteen

On Monday, I drove to Idaho Falls for the last two days of training for the body sculpting aesthetic spa. I was grateful we'd gotten moved into our new house. However, the financial stress was greater than ever. We had approximately $100 in our bank account, I still needed gas to get back to Boise, and we had a slew of bills. I couldn't be more ready to start this job.

While there, I learned the Meridian clinic was pushed back from opening yet again, not looking to open until the end of September. When I initially began speaking with them, it was August 1st.

I was stressing out. What were we going to do? How could I find money sooner?

I told one of the admins that I've been waiting on this job for a while, and it keeps being pushed back. I understand there is nothing you can do about it. It's all the red tape, etc., but it makes it very difficult for my family as it's another month before I see money, I said, the emotion in my voice apparent.

Feeling the truth in my words, she offered, "Maybe we can front you some money until then. Would that help?"

"Oh my God," I replied. "That'd be such a blessing. I'm also happy to come here and see patients before you open in Meridian, so I'm doing the work, and it's not being fronted."

"I'll see what I can find out," she responded.

I was very hopeful. It seemed another miracle was on its way.

A week later, on Monday, I hadn't received much of a response from Lauren, and I hadn't heard anything about any payment upfront. My intuition was screaming something didn't feel right. On Tuesday, she finally called me back.

"Hey, I wanted you to know, it looks like we're moving in a different direction. One of our doctors, who is already trained and has been doing this for years, has decided to move to Boise and will be taking the position instead."

"We want to help compensate you for your time and trouble and plan to send you $ 5,000."

I sat there shocked, not responding for a few seconds.

"OK," I replied, not knowing what else to say. "Thanks for letting me know."

"I hope this doesn't change our relationship," she responded.

"OK," I said.

Then I hung up the phone.

Wtf. I'd just lost another fucking job.

Another failure. This one was supposed to be foolproof.

Coming days after an evaluation with my trainer and one of the Belle admin staff members, they told me they thought I was great procedurally. Their one concern was that I was too "quiet" on my last day of training, and they wanted me to be a bit peppier with the clients. Something I wasn't concerned with, as I know I'm quiet when focused. And in this case, I was working to perfect the procedures. I knew that once I did them regularly, I'd be better able to converse throughout the process.

Regardless, it didn't matter. Another job bit the dust.

And down the vortex I went again.

My only saving grace was I'd be speaking at the International Conference of Integrative Medicine, ICIM, at the end of September on treating spike protein-related diseases, such as long-term covid and vaccine injuries, with frequency medicine. It was honestly one of the only things to keep me hanging on.

Please, God, I prayed, *let this be something for me.*

And it was, though, not what I was hoping for, an insight and/or opportunity to grow and make significant money. But it did provide me with colleagues who believed and felt the same way as I did, and there were many.

Two in particular come to mind, as both felt spiritually inspired to reach out, talk, and get to know me. One of the doctors asked that I join him for lunch following the end of the conference. It didn't take long after sitting that we both realized each other's deep spiritual connection. We immediately bonded, even swapping healing services with each other.

During his healing session with me he began to muscle test and asked several questions, one of which was asking my connection with God.

"Wow, you're God connection is testing really high, a 9/10. I don't believe I've ever seen anyone with that open a connection," he said.

"I'm also seeing a curse that was placed on your family. It goes back 6 generations on your Grandmother's side and is affecting your finances and ability to create financial abundance. Would you like to clear that?" He asked.

"100%!" I responded, "Please!"

He touched my forehead and a couple other areas and then muscle tested again, asking whether it had been cleared. I muscle tested yes.

In turn I helped the pain he'd been dealing with chronically in his left chest area and we both left each other feeling immensely better.

Returning from the conference, I quickly started looking for another job. I began asking around in my physician group, looking at all options. Within my physician group, I was directed to a new company called the Wellness Company, started by freedom fighters Dr. Ryan Cole, Dr. Peter McCullough, and Dr. Harvey Risch, among others.

The Wellness Company is a virtual telehealth company providing acute sick appointments, medical exemption letters, and long-term/preventative care. Surely, it would provide me with the additional income we needed to pay our bills every month.

By mid-November, all credentialing was done, and I was set for availability and appointments starting the week of Thanksgiving. I was looking forward to finally having additional cash in our bank account and less stress in my body.

Unfortunately, the Universe had other plans. For the entirety of the week, I took care of two patients and made $60 total. The following week, nothing. At some point around that time, I was made aware they'd be offering exemption letters, to which I enthusiastically responded, *Yes*, I'm available.

Yes, I thought, *this is perfect*. I'll write a lot of letters, which will bring in money.

But alas, anytime I responded and/or signed up for a full week of call and availability, I'd receive no work.

The month of December was quickly passing, and this new job wasn't providing much of anything to help. More than that, I was supposed to go to Costa Rica for work, but at this time, there was absolutely no money for that trip.

I believe the change started fully when I lost the Belle Medical job. It felt like the last nail in the coffin, and I felt a significant shift in my mindset and mood. I lost all trust I'd ever succeed.

Bodhi seemed a distant past, and I began the thought process of how it should end, focusing only on the job that would finally provide and end the stress we'd been living under for the last three years. To do this, I felt inclined to make my Quantal U series public for the first time without charging anything for them. They'd been watched on average only ten times, and at the very least, people should have access. Maybe they'll help someone eventually.

My vision and dream of growing a worldwide integrative website was over. And, I saw little, if any, hope for things to change, sinking into a numb, flat existence.

I no longer focused on my vision of integrative therapies. My only focus was having a job and a stable income. I honestly didn't care about anything else. I was *done* with my family suffering. I was done feeling guilty and shameful I couldn't make it work, couldn't make it succeed.

I was giving up and acquiescing, "This *must* be the experience I'm supposed to have, as no matter what I do, I fail."

And if I were Jesus, holding vast amounts of knowledge, experience, wisdom, and expertise, doesn't it go without saying I should be able to manifest some money?

The thoughts kept circling. It was the same circus but a different show.

Again, and again, and again.

Adding further insult to injury, the medical director job in Bend was over at the end of December. The owner had difficulties with the landlord of her building, who forced her to close the doors.

My fourth lost job in one year.

Done.

Done.

Done.

Even with the financial stress, Christmas 2022 was lean but successful.

For myself included.

As a lover of gift-giving, Taylor collaborated with her sisters and Brian to buy me a beautiful stone lamp.

And with Brian's insurance job, he had close to $1200 in his mileage program with AIL. As one of my Christmas presents, Brian used his mileage to purchase my ticket to Costa Rica. Without that, there was no way I could go.

My kids and knight in shining armor came through, a bright spot at a time when most everything else in my career and finances felt bleak.

I was going to Costa Rica for work, and while there, I would be participating in my first plant medicine ceremony in a group. I'm a huge advocate for this type of experience and know that, for many, the biggest healing work can happen under the influence of psychedelic plants.

Plant medicine helps us bypass the reticular endothelial system, our conscious systems, opening us to different frequencies, levels of consciousness, and creating new neural synapses. It helps us "tap in" easier, get answers to difficult problems, and helps energetically clear limiting beliefs and/or patterns that are causing issues in our lives. And its now becoming one of the leading therapies in treating PTSD, depression, anxiety, and other forms of mental health.

My intention was two-fold. First, I needed unyielding proof of the things I'd channeled about myself and the people I've been, as I'd lost all focus and trust in myself.

Secondly, I felt done.

More than anything, I was *done*. A phrase that came over and over. "I'm done."

Done.

Done.

I wouldn't harm myself, but I felt no drive nor push toward anything anymore. Finding a job was the priority and at the forefront of my time, efforts, and focus.

And I wanted this feeling of *done-ness* to go away.

Thankfully, Costa Rica and the plant experience were everything I'd hoped for and more.

I fell in love with the people, the countryside, the simplicity, the incredible beauty, and the numerous animals available to see.

I filled my cup with Mother Earth's beauty, looking for epic photo ops and the chance to connect and just *be*.

We saw trees of swinging monkeys, sloths, millions of adorable sand crabs, beautiful birds, and the largest rattlesnake I've ever seen.

And we visited healthcare and wellness centers and looked at several potential properties worth buying.

I also met wonderful new people, physicians and practitioners with whom I could see myself working in the future.

All in all, it was the trip of a lifetime.

The most impactful being the plant medicine experience.

We arrived at the retreat center Con Smania on a late Thursday afternoon, our ceremony planned for the next day.

The retreat center is a beautiful escape, consisting of several eclectic buildings and housing that include a pool and waterslide, make-your-own juice bar, an airplane hangar (used for ceremonies), and a large house/building for classes, yoga, breath work, or other.

I was sharing a room with Crystal Dawn, a beautiful black, spiritual physician-goddess of a woman. We were introduced by the trip planner, Charlotte Gibbons, and had met a year earlier on the phone and in person for the first time on this trip. Crystal Dawn was as unique as they come, especially for a physician. And I loved everything about her.

Following her intuition, she began experimenting with plant medicine 15-20 years earlier, a pioneer in the use and advancement of psychedelic plants for healing reasons and purposes. Now, she travels the world over seeking spiritual opportunities, medical missions, meditation retreats, plant medicine experiences, and visits hot springs.

I thoroughly enjoyed getting to know her on this trip and was happy to share a room.

Before the ceremony, I paid a healer $50 to muscle test and assess areas I may be blocked or whether I was carrying any negative energies that may impact or affect the ceremony. I sat down next to her, and for the next few minutes, she was muscle testing. In the end, she determined I had no entities, but I had every other block, including, and most importantly, I was muscle testing, as *done*.

Done.

Done.

Done.

She was happy to clear it for me...for another $550.

The ceremony was set to begin at noon, with a breathwork class starting around 10 AM. For best results, it was recommended that everyone fast or at least stick to easy-to-digest foods such as fruit or a smoothie.

We did breath work first, something I love, helping to bring us energetically into better focus.

There were approximately 20 people in the group, and we were situated in a circle, each of us with a twin-sized mattress.

We went in a circle, taking turns introducing ourselves and discussing our intentions. Many of us cried, myself included. But even then, I couldn't fully express what I was hoping for in this experience. It felt too raw, too sensitive, and too vulnerable.

"Hey there. My name is Elisa Peavey, I'm a physician, and I am from Idaho. The last couple of years, I've struggled, trying to figure out who I am and what I'm supposed to do," I said, my voice quivering.

"My intention is to seek and know with more clarity my purpose," I said, making the same basic statement as the majority of those in the ceremony. As there was no way I would say, I want absolute *knowing* I'm Princess Diana, Elizabeth Taylor, Joan of Arc, and most importantly... Jesus Christ."

They'd have all looked at me like I was crazy. Because even with all the synchronicities and other circumstantial evidence towards that statement, I'd lost about 90% faith that any of it was actually true. I felt crazy, especially as *everything* in my life was going wrong and getting worse.

I'd lost faith that Bodhi would amount to anything. And my idea of having an international site with eons of information, science, and access to holistic physicians, practitioners, intuitives, psychics, vibrational sound therapists, and more were lost. I didn't have the finances to pay the yearly domain fee, let alone the monthly maintenance and educational videos.

Every psychic or intuitive healer I'd worked with told me the same thing: it would happen.

But when? And at what cost? I had no confidence in myself anymore. Everything I did never amounted to anything.

Every class, every offering, every Bodhi special. I couldn't even get people to watch a free video series.

I felt beyond broken, and I was desperately searching for definitive confirmation.

The facilitator then handed me my medicine. I was ready.

We took our medicine at the same time, each person with a unique combination depending on their wants, intentions, and potential reactions to it. After we were asked to lay on the mattress, ethereal music began playing loudly over the speakers, alternating with sound therapy, crystal bowls, and singing.

Beside us were eye masks, which the facilitator asked us to place over our eyes when we felt the medicine start working.

I closed my eyes and waited for it to kick in.

My facilitator chose a combination of medicines that would first open the heart, followed by ones that would facilitate more of a spiritual connection. He had intuited, as I was in instant tears during our pre-medicine conversation, that I needed to start there first.

After what felt like forever and not "feeling" anything, I was getting frustrated. I began going over the intentions I'd written in my notebook, the first of which was needing confirmation.

The reality of it hitting me squarely, like a punch to the gut.

"I don't TRUST IT!" I screamed in my head, bursting into tears and sobbing. I'm DONE!!!!

I don't believe it. Everything I've done has failed, and every attempt to make money not working.

How can I be expected to get anywhere when all I get is fucked, over and over? It's impossible!

I don't trust anything anymore, I thought.

And then I simply heard, "I Am."

Suddenly Jesus was before me, a circle of light between my abdomen/chest and his, holding the both of us connected and facing one another.

With the repetitive thought coming over and over, *I Am.*

I Am.

I Am.

I Am.

It kept coming over and over.

I Am.

I Am.

I Am.

I was sobbing, the intensity of the emotion and confirmation coursing through me so big I felt the need to place my hand over my heart, offering support.

I Am.

"I Really Am," I began saying in my head, huge tears pouring down my face.

I Am.

I Am.

As the words kept repeating and I continued to say them in my head, the circle of light between myself and Jesus began to grow, intensify, and expand, strengthening our bond and connection.

After an unknown period of time, I saw several of my other lives. Each of them following the same process as Jesus.

"I Am," I said with Elizabeth Taylor. Seeing and understanding the massive impact she had on the AIDS community. Seeing and understanding the karma she agreed to play out in that life, from her health issues to her multiple marriages to her addictions. Incredible amounts of loss and pain.

"I Am," I said with Princess Diana. Seeing and understanding her massive impact on humanitarian efforts around the world. Seeing that she carried the same healing gift as I do with her hands.

The same gift Jesus carried.

I Am. I said about Joan of Arc. Seeing and understanding her incredible ability to channel and act as a direct conduit to God.

I Am.

I Am.

I Am.

The feeling was all-encompassing and everything I'd been asking for.

The "I Am" thoughts began to subside. At some point, the facilitator came and asked how I was doing, checking to see if I was ready or wanted to start the next medicine.

I was, and he brought me 2.5 grams of psilocybin chocolate. After eating, I went back into my process.

I saw colors upon colors, as well as multiple geometrical symbols. I saw that both Bella and Emi were carrying or holding some of my stuff.

Let it go, I said as I watched the heavier energy clear them both.

At one point, I saw a snake, straight as a rod. I immediately thought, "The snake is medicine."

And then, I am the snake.

Wait. I Am the medicine.

Then I saw an elephant, and the thought came, "Wisdom."

Then, I'm the Wisdom! I realized

I bring the wisdom and the medicine. I'm both.

The string of thoughts was coming fast and furious.

I Am.

I Am.

I Am.

Over and over.

The experience flew by, and eight hours later, when the ceremony ended, I was enveloped in immense gratitude, the feeling enveloping my body completely.

Thank you, I kept saying over and over. By this time, I was sitting on my mattress, my hands firmly clasped together in prayer.

Thank you.

Thank you.

Thank you, God.

The experience was everything I needed and more.

Afterward, instead of joining the others, I returned to my room to take it all in.

The next morning, I felt different, lighter. The bleak fog I'd been under felt like it was lifting a bit.

I actually felt like conversing and getting to know the other people for the first time since I'd arrived.

More importantly, I'd received the confirmation I desperately wanted and needed.

I definitively knew who I was and who I'd been.

I knew I had work still to do here, though I had no idea how it would come about.

And oddly, I knew and realized I was still feeling done. The incongruencies between "knowing" who I've been vs. the loss of passion or motive to create anything created divisive and difficult thoughts.

How was I to reconcile this? As I certainly wasn't paying $550 for someone to shift my "doneness" to "motivation and readiness," I couldn't afford it.

A week later, I was back in the States, preparing to speak at a fundraiser called Intra Life Healing Arts, where I had joined the board a year earlier.

It was Intra Life's first fundraiser as it was still in its infancy, only two years old. It started when the CEO channeled the vision to create a non-profit to bring integrative and mind/body healing therapies to clinics and health systems throughout the Treasure Valley. She started the pilot program at a place called Lotus Tree, a business offering multiple therapeutic options for kids with learning disabilities, sensitivities, and those on the spectrum.

It was so successful that Intra Life had contracted with the local women's and children's shelter and another clinic system at the time of the fundraiser.

It's everything I believe is the future of medicine, where I often envision the use of energy-frequency devices, medical intuitives, and energy healers as part of the medical team.

Imagine a traumatic motor vehicle accident. The victim comes in with multiple wounds but is also dealing with the shock and emotional aftermath of the trauma itself. Imagine a world where we have the people and the skills necessary to immediately help them process and release the emotional impact so it doesn't stay stuck, causing PTSD or other long-term medical and physical ailments or problems.

This was everything Intra Life was working to create and bring to the Treasure Valley, and I was all for it.

Chapter Fifteen

I was speaking with Dr. Higginbotham, one of Boise's first pioneers in the world of emotional and mind/body health. My Dad completed a rotation with him in 1992, and in 2010, 18 years later, I also completed a rotation with him. The impact he had on my Dad was great enough to inspire me to do one as well.

To say it was the most inspiring rotation of my medical career would be a massive understatement. In just two weeks, Dr. Higginbotham completely changed my idea of what medicine could be. I'd been rotating through traditional medicine practices and in-services, all following the typical rubric of do more, see more, treat more, and get more; the hamster wheel of 10-15 minute appointments to diagnose and treat.

But Dr. Higginbotham was different. His appointments were at least an hour, sometimes longer. And his patients didn't come and sit on a chair while he took a history and asked questions. Instead, they'd lay on his OMM (Osteopathic Manipulative Medicine) table, and he'd start asking the patient questions while muscle testing. During my rotation, he had a couple of medical intuitives working with and helping him identify areas of the body that were impacted and/or to '*see*' anything else that may be happening with the patient.

A medical intuitive is one who can energetically see where there are areas of dysfunction within the body, and will often know what's needed to clear, treat, or energetically fix the underlying problem. One of the medical intuititives working with Dr. Higginbotham was Ashiauna, the founder and CEO of Intra Life Healing Arts.

I watched people enter his office in severe pain and walk out virtually pain-free. His method was simply locating the underlying emotion and/or cause of a particular symptom through muscle testing, medical intuitive insight, and asking the right questions. Whether it was a hormonal issue, a liver problem, chronic muscular pain, or even an autoimmune disease, he was often able to find the root cause and work on healing it.

They didn't all walk out completely healed, but several did and or had significant improvement in their pain and low mood. I'd never seen anything like it.

The traditional medical system has three options to treat *dis-ease*: medication, talk therapy, and surgery.

Forget about searching for, finding, and treating the root cause. Instead, its main focus was pushing medications for everything.

Have an autoimmune disease? No problem, take this hard-core medicine, which will also decrease your immune system response and increase your risk of developing numerous infections instead of finding the root cause of *why* the disease has presented in the first place.

Have a low thyroid? No problem. Instead of looking at anti-inflammatory foods and underlying emotional causes, we'll treat with synthetic thyroid hormone, a tedious and often difficult task to manage as thyroid levels are chaotic and all over the place.

Which is exactly what doctors do every day, instead of fixing the underlying reason for *why* it developed in the first place.

For example, take the case of a young woman with a low thyroid. While thyroid issues can and do impact men and women, most sufferers are women with certain characteristics, as the thyroid is linked to the throat chakra and the triple warmer meridian. The throat chakra is our area of self-expression and personal power. When our triple warmer is underactive, we begin to feel heaviness and fatigue, and we can start to show signs of depression. Typically, those afflicted aren't using their voice or speaking their truth. And most often, they've put themselves on the back burner for years and years, putting everyone else on the forefront. Not only do they become physically and energetically fatigued and exhausted, they're often unable to fill their own cup as everything they have to give is given away to others.

I know this all too well because my thyroid went caput, regardless of how well I ate or how much I exercised. I couldn't keep the weight from coming on, and the fatigue, mental fog, and low energy were off the charts. In fact, I'm fairly certain it was my low thyroid that predisposed me and led to my injury in January 2016.

At the time, I'd been doing CrossFit (CF) since 2012, and though not the strongest, I was a good athlete. But for some reason, from the time I moved to Bend on October 20, 2015, until late January, something significant happened to me. I'd gained 10-15 lbs in two months, and whenever I'd go to CF, it felt like I was moving through mud. My muscles had difficulty recovering, and each class caused significant soreness for days. A week or two leading up to my injury, I consciously chose to stay at my new job, one I'd recently come to learn, I hated.

Instead of doing what I really wanted, which was bringing energy and other integrative therapies into medicine. Being that bridge.

But it didn't matter, as I was my family's main source of income, and I needed to guarantee continued financial stability.

From an emotional standpoint, I was stifling my truth and what I believed I should be doing to financially survive. And my thyroid took the hit.

If I'd seen Dr. Higginbotham for it, he'd have gotten to the underlying emotional reason my thyroid wasn't happy. He is a true pioneer, paving the way for integrative therapies to become mainstream, and I was beyond ecstatic to share the stage.

Unfortunately, the night was clouded with this feeling of *doneness*, directly contradicting who I *knew* myself to be.

I still felt *done*. And all I wanted to do was cry.

I met Ashi, the CEO of Intra Life, a week later for coffee to catch up on the event and touch base since I'd been in Costa Rica. That morning, in the shower, I asked God to please have her tell me whatever I most needed to hear since she was a gifted medical intuitive and medium.

How was I to reconcile what I knew of myself and my purpose with the fact that I felt done and was having a hard time finding much, if anything, positive about what I would soon be doing for work?

Because all I'd wanted was for Bodhi to succeed, and now I'm heading back into the same traditional medical system I left three years ago. It was broken, unethical, and often immoral... then.

I can only assume the hit it's taken since the pandemic.

It doesn't have the patients, staff, or my best interest at heart, as traditional medicine is unfortunately controlled by insurance companies, lobbyists, and pharmaceutical companies whose intent and purpose are money and control. They want us sick. When we're sick, we're consumers. When healthy, they don't make money.

They are businesses, and their bottom dollar is all that matters.

The '*do more, see more, get more*' model is burning out physicians faster than any other professional career. Add that to the epidemic of physician suicide that has exponentially risen in mass proportions, and it's obvious the system doesn't work effectively.

For anyone.

And now I'm going back into it for the sake of my family and for our financial stability.

And I was done.

"Please, Ashi, what do I need to hear today?" I said to myself as I walked in to see her.

"Hey!" she said, sliding me a thank you note, her face beaming her beautiful Ashi smile. "How's it going?"

"Doing OK," I said, smiling back.

We discussed how Intra Life did at the fundraiser and discussed what we know to do differently for the next one.

"And as soon as we get more donations, we can start searching for a clinic for you," Ashi said.

Immediately, I felt tears come to my eyes as working full time plus would leave little time for anything else.

"Ashi, I'm not sure I have the bandwidth or the time to put towards that. I am in the process of getting another job or two, and I'm worried I'll be spread too thin. But I want you to know that I 100% believe in the intention and purpose of Intra Life, and I will continue to support you however I can," I said, tears rolling down my face.

"OK," she replied. "Whatever you need."

Looking deep into my eyes, her concern was evident on her face.

I hadn't wanted to talk with her about this, but it suddenly started coming.

"For the last three years, I have been experiencing downloads and information about myself and the people I've been. I've felt impressed to learn all these lives as I felt they were pertinent to my purpose in this lifetime."

I stopped for a moment and looked at her.

"I've channeled that I was Joan of Arc," I said, pausing.

"And Princess Diana."

"And Elizabeth Taylor."

I paused.

"And Jesus Christ," I whispered, looking at my hands.

"And when I had the plant experience, my intention was to definitively know the truth of those lives."

"And I have that. I don't doubt who I've been anymore," I said.

"I truly believe."

I paused again.

"But the problem is I have this inner contradiction as all I feel is...done," I said as I looked again into her eyes, tears pouring down my face.

"How do I resolve this?" I asked.

"Go, do you," Ashi said. "All you need to do is spend some time with you, loving you. And it will shift."

"And I'm also seeing, *whoooph*, yeah, this is big. You need to psychically protect yourself," she added.

I looked up, shocked. I didn't feel I had any attachments and was checked for that before my plant ceremony. Not having an attachment was the only thing I had going for me.

"I see something behind you. Not sure when it got there. There's also something in your husband's office. It comes through his computer. It's brought in because of his financial fear. He needs to understand how to block it."

"And it messes with you at night while you're sleeping," she continued.

"And I'm seeing something in your bathroom? I believe it was there before you moved in. It messes with your daughter."

"Emi?" I asked.

"Yes, she's the youngest? I see bright and shiny for your older two, but I see her with her arms across her chest. She carries a lot of generational shame. You two are passing it back and forth."

I couldn't believe it. She confirmed what I'd been feeling, that Emi was carrying some of my stuff energetically.

"OK, this is big. You really need to hear this. You have to block and clear. Call in Archangel Michael and clear your house and your space every morning and every night. Take Michael and envision he is wrapping his wings around you and keeping everything else out."

"You and your family are being inundated with psychic energies that are making it very difficult to do what you need to," she continued.

"This is very important for you," she said.

"And," she said, looking me squarely in the eyes again. "I am being told it will happen. Everything you'd envisioned will happen. Your guide is firmly telling me."

"It will happen. Trust the process."

"If only it were that easy," I said, laughing.

"Thank you, Ashi. This conversation was everything," I added.

Most importantly, it reiterated the importance of keeping our auric and ethereal Fields clear from unwanted psychic energies.

Our existence is multi-dimensional, and even on Earth, though you may not see them, we are inundated by psychic energies, entities, and other influences every day. Becoming aware of this fact and learning to keep yourself clear is one of the most important tools you can have. For your health, your emotions, and for better coherence.

This was a huge aspect of Jesus's work. He often healed those who were sick simply by clearing their ethereal and auric systems from negative entities.

This is a lesson I learned all too well with Taylor, and one I believe she agreed to experience for me to realize the absolute importance of this in our day-to-day lives. Our experience as a family is why I feel so compelled to help other families, kids, and parents in similar situations. And why I feel it necessary to educate and teach others how to psychically protect themselves.

Around that time, I felt more impressed than ever to write a book and share my experiences. I'd had the impulse before, but this was much stronger, and the ideas were pouring in. I decided to give it a try, and I sat down to write.

Unlike before, the book organization and planning began flowing through me. Before I knew it, I had 50 pages written in a matter of days. Most of the time, it occurred while in the shower: images, memories, ideas, and ways to organize, flowing in wave after wave.

I was also applying for several new jobs. One as a medical director at a prison in Arizona, one as a medical director for an IV bar, and the other working at a Women's and Obstetrics Center in Oregon.

And, unless something unprecedented occurs, at the time of writing this book, I'm working full time at a Women's and Obstetrics clinic, delivering babies again. Something I truly loved, cherished, and have missed these last few years. It also provides my family with a consistent and guaranteed monthly income, for which I am incredibly grateful.

In addition, I get to use many of the intuitive and hands-on healing gifts and the wisdom and knowledge I've cultivated and grown over the last several years in regards to plant medicine, essential oils, sound and vibratory therapy, and other integrative therapies; allowing me to better care for my patients. This includes the use of several new tools advanced in the technology of frequency medicine, or better said, tapping into the Zero Point Field.

I'm not entirely sure what God has in store for me. I don't know how or what, but I can guarantee it won't be anything I expect, so I'm doing my best to let go of expectations.

I don't know why my family and I had to go through such a difficult experience of financial lack.

I don't know why it was necessary.

But because of that experience, I am a completely different person and my family is completely different too. And I've learned a lot, for which I'm beyond grateful.

I used to think I was a good cook before, now I'm a damn good cook.

Where I didn't know how to spend less than $1500/month on food, I can now make $300 last for several weeks, cooking the majority of food from scratch; using vegetables, onions, garlic, potatoes, and rice as the main staples.

When my girls say there's no food in the house, I'll make you a heart-healthy and heart-warming meal.

A skill I'm incredibly grateful to have.

I'm also more grounded, centred, present, patient, calm and balanced and I can feel it in the way I interact with others and in the way I feel about myself.

Most importantly, I am beyond proud and grateful for my family. They, too, have been through the wringer of pain and growth in the last several years, whether they understood it or not.

They felt, suffered, and wondered whether we'd make it too.

But make it we did. We are truly closer than ever. The relationships between my girls are supportive and loving. Something I never thought possible.

And I can tell you this.

I know with certainty who I am and who I've been.

I know I am a skilled conduit and healer whose gift will continue to grow.

I know I am a master of Zero Point energy, and I will continue to grow my skill of that mastery in my ISR, avatar life, as Elisa.

Through the Zero Point Field, I work closely with God, Archangel Michael, my sister Windy, my guides, and others in the multi-dimensional realm to clear negative energies from spaces, people, and places.

I work with them to help my patients heal.

And to heal myself.

I also know my personal purpose.

My personal and spiritual purpose is mastery and ascension in this life. And my job is to "tap in," remembering the soul skills, tools, and knowledge I need for my personal advancement and ascension.

I *am* Elisa, the divine feminine, *twin-soul* to Jesus of Nazareth, the divine masculine.

I'm not a success.

I'm imperfect. I make many mistakes, and I'll make plenty more before I ascend the Earth plane.

But as Jesus whispered to me in a recent shower meditation.

I'll get there *in spite* of me. In spite of being too much, too emotional, too stubborn, too impatient, too broke inside, too imperfect, a failure, not smart enough, not confident enough, too quick to assume, too hard on myself, too, too, too...

I'll get there *in spite* of me. And also *because* of me.

I have my multi-dimensional team of rockstars and a slew of people who love and support me.

And I feel very certain I'll get there.

Recently I've been seeing groupings of 1111's the last several days, indicating something new would be revealed.

This morning on 4/20/23 at exactly 11:11, I was alerted to my phone. The alert was a YouTube tarot reading from Mystic Monroe, asking of the tarot cards, "What does your *higher self* have in store for you?" where the watcher chooses one of three piles from which to receive a group reading. I picked pile number two. Here was that read.

Joseph Moon, the tarot reader: "The Empress, that is what I was feeling. I do feel there is a little bit of sadness, though, so there could have been a loss, or there could have been something where you need to be easier on yourself. It feels like the new beginning is your family and having this new sense of pride. That is the end result. What will happen to you is that you'll be so proud of yourself. You've done it. You've started something new. You've literally birthed something new into the world. It also has a lot to do with your tradition, something to connect to your tradition. Your ancestors are bringing through this energy for you. So, I do feel that you need to know, let yourself have compassion for yourself, and be really easy on yourself.

Let yourself receive the light. That is going to be very important. Connecting and getting outside into the sunshine. Give that love to the plants. Doing that activity will do that for your body. So, you are also believing in yourself. So, getting it out, saying it to a plant, you say it back to yourself.

You already know what you have within you. You already have the tools. From what you've learned in past experiences, know you can do this. Your fear is "I don't want to go through another challenge, like I don't want to go through any more sadness, or like have anything that dims the light, and you need to sort of take off that shell and believe in yourself again because um, what I'm picking up the most is that, whoever that is, your partner in crime, they're going to be there for you in this next phase. Umm, the personal growth stuff is sort of over now, I'm hearing. It's always there, but it's not the personal growth at the level of sadness you've had in the past.

The Tower; this is in the past. Showing whatever was happening before was kind of scary, and a lot of traumatic stuff happened. It really affected you, but now you have to trust that things will be OK this time. That's what I'm getting. Because I feel strongly that the end result is that you will be so proud of yourself. Because the new beginning that's coming for you is you're sticking to believing in the end result, being whatever it is.

Also, I feel like this new journey will completely change your life very quickly. Lots of things you might be doing now will change. Yes, Ten of Swords. A lot of old habits and old things will die quickly. And it won't be a negative thing.

Don't hold on to the past. OK?

Ace of Cups, showing very strongly that you worked on yourself, you had to go through that, and your cup is now full. New beginning card. Your cup is now full. You don't need to do any more healing or self-evaluation or looking at things on a deep level. You just need to get back out into the sunshine, soaking up and being and feeling abundant in yourself. Also, looking after your skin and nourishing yourself with things that make you feel good. Like herbs and stuff, aromatherapy and stuff you enjoy.

These are the things you want to do, not the deep, deep dive, like the tarot reading, "What do I need to do today?" All you need to do is keep treating yourself the way you feel you deserve to be treated.

King of Pentacles, OK. Someone. This King of Pentacles is also, like I said, your partner in crime, King of Pentacles. They're going to somehow be very, very stable and have all the things you need. Also, if you are doing a product or creating something and you're working with someone, they're going to have everything you need to support you to create that product.

I hope that makes sense.

The Nine of Swords. Block out. Block it all out. These thoughts that you keep in your head sometimes, these fears of wondering, "Am I doing it right?" Umm...being a perfectionist about everything. You need to let that go. Past failures. That's how we create limiting beliefs; something goes wrong, and we think, "I can't do that again" because we think it's going to go wrong. But because it went wrong then, it doesn't mean it will go wrong again, that you will fail again. Saying, "I can't do this, I can't do that, this could be something that stops me, or I would feel really bad if I do that again." Don't let that dampen your style, OK? Keep being who you truly feel in your heart.

Every journey is different. When a new project comes, it's a completely new project, a new child. So don't limit yourself to thinking I have to do it like this,

this this. We are not AI robots. We are humans. We are creative. We work with the energy that comes from tapping into what your heart wants to choose. What is the vibrational flow choosing for you to do?

Just let it all go, stop thinking about it, stop panicking. Everything will be good. OK?"

His tarot read was resonating with me on every level, in every way. Further confirming that simply trusting in, believing in, and loving me is how I'll get there. It was as if the read was directed at me and me only.

I truly believe that ascension is mine.

Most importantly, I get to help millions of others along the way.

Here, I Am.

Gratitude

At the top of the list of people in my life that I am grateful for is my husband Brian who has supported me in ways unfathomable to most. He took on most of the housework, dishes, child caregiving, cooking, and more for the majority of our years while I was attending medical school and in residency. I hardly remember a time coming home from a weekend moonlighting or a month away for rotations when the house wasn't cleaned, or our girls weren't happy. With his love of language and always giving and doing for others, Brian has always gone out of his way to do as much as he can for me, whenever he can. He has selflessly sent me on rest and renewal trips when he knew how much I needed it, often putting himself last. There are so many things I'm forever and eternally grateful to him. Most importantly, Brian is and has always been the epitome of what a good Dad should be. He goes out of his way to make sure his girls are taken care of, taking the time for homework, car trips, volunteering as a soccer coach, taxi driver, late night running to friends' home, or hanging and playing fortnight with them and their friends. No matter what, he lives for his girls and his family. Thank you, Brian, for everything you've done and will continue to do for me, our girls, and our family.

To my oldest Taylor. Thank you, thank you, thank you! You have been my biggest source of learning and growth for which I'm forever grateful. Thank you for your strength and for your courage. Thank you for agreeing to experience the gummy and difficult moments in order for me to learn what my soul needed. I'm beyond proud of the human you're becoming and know you will and already are, changing the world. Love you, T!

To my daughter, Isabella Grace. From the moment you were born, I was in awe of you. I kept staring at you following your beautiful delivery. You were perfect, empowering me to the point I wanted to do it all over again. You are my grace and the calm between storms. Thank you for being *you*, for allowing me the grace I needed, even if I didn't deserve it. I am beyond proud to be your Mom and thank you for choosing me for this life experience, know you'll accomplish *big* things. Love you Boo!

To Miss Emi Peavey, my baby, our caboose. Thank you for being *you*, and for coming into our world with a *bang!* You're the perfect completion and complement to our family. Without you, we wouldn't be. Your wisdom, compassion, and your ability to sense and see the illusion around you is so beautiful. Thank you for loving me. Thank you for believing in my healing abilities and having the absolute *knowing* that I'll always help you feel better. It's been a wonderful blessing.

To my Mom and my Number One fan, I love you. The gratitude I have for you would fill the oceans as you have always been there for me. And not just for me but for all your children, and all your family, and all your friends, and for anyone else who needs it. You are the epitome of unconditional, non-judgmental love, giving it as freely as others will allow. Whether it be helping a struggling family financially or simply taking the time to look them in the eyes and let them know how much you appreciate them. You go out of your way to let others feel and know your love. Mom, you are my rock, my right hand, my confidant, my person. Thank you for always being there. Thank you for loving and believing in *me*. It is because of you that I learned God was someone we can talk to. It is because of you that I realized there was a different way to do medicine, and it's because of you I am here. I am eternally grateful for everything you are and everything you do for humanity.

To my Dad, my idol. You're the Number One person to whom I measure everything, always wanting to be just like you. I watched you do hard things and knew I could do them too. I observed the sacrifices you made over the years and knew I could make them as well. I observed the compassion and love you have for your patients, and I wanted to exhibit the same. Your heart, honesty, integrity, goodness, and undying devotion to your family is *beyond*. Some of my fondest memories are working alongside you as a colleague and learning from you. Thank you, Dad, for always loving me, supporting me, and believing in me.

To my beautiful friend and colleague, Michele Cox. Thank you for listening to your intuition to reach out, and knowing we needed to meet and become friends. We have known each other through millennia, of this I'm certain. Thank you for being my friend and thank you for seeing *me*. Most importantly, thank you for supporting my journey, reading my rough drafts, and giving your intuitive thoughts and feedback. You have a beautiful soul, and I am forever grateful our paths came together. I look forward to our continued friendship and collaboration, for years to come.

To Ron Gaber, former Dean of Students at ATSU-KCOM, thank you for always believing and supporting me and my family throughout the years. Your belief in me helped me believe in myself and I'm forever grateful.

To my brother Doug and his husband Anthony. Thank you for always being there and for loving and supporting our family through thick and thin. Your hearts, compassion, and generosity are inspirational. Love you both *beyond*.

To my beautiful sister Windy. So much to say. More than anything: I love you, I love you, I love you! And I am so grateful for you in my life. I feel closer to you than I ever did when you were alive, your ethereal impact and presence in my life is felt on a monumental level. Thank you for agreeing to your departure in this life in order to help guide and support us from the other side. Without a doubt, I know it was part of the experience you agreed to have for a variety of important reasons. Your boys will always know how incredibly special and amazing their Mama was, of that we will make sure. See you when we meet again. XOXO.